THE

VEGAN

BEAN

Cookbook

THE
VEGAN
BEAN
Cookbook

High-Protein, Plant-Based Meals
That Are Better *for* Your Body, Schedule *and* Budget

Andrea Soranidis

Founder of The Petite Cook and author of *20-Minute Italian*

PAGE STREET
PUBLISHING CO.

PAGE STREET
PUBLISHING CO.

First published in 2021 by

Page Street Publishing Co.

27 Congress Street, Suite 105

Salem, MA 01970

www.pagestreetpublishing.com

Distributed by Macmillan, sales in Canada by The Canadian Manda Group.

25   24   23   22   21   1   2   3   4   5

ISBN-13: 978-1-64567-385-9

ISBN-10: 1-64567-385-5

Library of Congress Control Number: 2021931340

Cover and book design by Rosie Stewart for Page Street Publishing Co.

Photography by Andrea Soranidis

Printed and bound in China

Contents

Introduction

Welcome to *The Vegan Bean Cookbook*!

I'm so excited you decided to pick up this cookbook! Brace yourself, because we are about to start a journey into the bean world. Believe me, you'll be amazed by how many things you can do with these tiny little powerhouses. If you've ever thought that beans are boring, I'm here to change your mind with these vegan bean recipes for everything from lasagna, meatless loaf and tacos to curries, frittatas and sandwiches, and yes, even desserts! Well, especially desserts!

Beans are inexpensive, easy to find and loaded with plant-based protein and lots of other healthy goodness. I mean, what's not to love?

When I first started incorporating more beans into my cooking—both for my blog, The Petite Cook, and in my daily diet—I didn't have a clue. I would spend hours on the internet or flicking through my cookbooks trying to find delicious ways to cook with beans. I won't lie—it was a challenge! That's why I decided to put together a cookbook that featured all my favorite classic recipes made easier and bean-loaded!

The 60 recipes in this book will show you just how easy it is to build meals from legumes for your daily menu. Some recipes take as little as twenty minutes to make, such as the No-Tuna Chickpea Salad Sandwich (page 118) and Asian-Style Mixed Bean Lettuce Wraps (page 31), and they are perfect lunchbox options. Others are traditional dishes cleverly turned plant-based, like the Classic Family Meat(less)loaf (page 24) and The Ultimate Vegan Shepherd's Pie (page 15). These two recipes are perfect proof that you don't have to give up familiar flavors to embrace a meat-free lifestyle.

And let's not forget about the desserts! I know you might be a bit skeptical when you bite into your first bean-based dessert, but I promise you, it will leave you completely astonished. Desserts with a pulse addition not only taste delicious, but they also have a welcome nutritional boost, so it's a win-win situation! Start with the Black Bean Chocolate Pudding (page 143) and the Butter Bean-licious Cookie Dough (page 135) and go from there. Trust me, once you give bean-based desserts a try, you'll be making them over and over again.

I'm not a fan of labels in general, especially when it comes to dietary beliefs. Therefore, I didn't create these recipes just for vegans, but for anyone who wants to incorporate more plant-forward recipes in their daily diet. Whether you're newly looking to reduce your animal-product consumption or you have already adopted a plant-based lifestyle, I'm here to help you discover how beans can help you through your journey.

I was new to the plant-based world myself when I started crafting these vegan bean recipes, and I wanted to make this cookbook as accessible as possible, so I focused on just legumes rather than other well-known vegan protein sources, like tofu, tempeh and seitan. However, most of the recipes are incredibly versatile, and you will find it pretty easy to add in some crumbled tofu, tempeh or seitan in the curries, stews and salads featured in this book, if you'd like. And you are most definitely welcome to add a sprinkle of nutritional yeast or vegan cheese to the pasta recipes or even into the omelet and frittata recipes featured here.

Before you start trying the delicious recipes in this cookbook, make sure you read the Ingredient Tips section on page 10. You'll find some really useful advice to help you make the most of these dishes. Most of the time, you'll be able to use canned or dried beans interchangeably without affecting the final result. However, there are a couple of recipes that specifically tell you to go for dried beans, so trust me in those instances. I've most definitely tested them with the canned version, and they didn't work out well! If you've never cooked with dried beans before, you'll find a little helpful guide on page 11.

Ultimately, I hope you'll use this book as a creative outlet to gather the inspiration you need to embrace more beans in your life. Pulses can do so much more than merely act as an extra add-on in soups and salads—they can easily turn a classic dish into an exciting, protein-packed meal.

Most importantly, remember to have fun in the kitchen—happy cooking!

Andrea ♥

Ingredient Tips

To make the most of this cookbook, I've put together a few helpful tips that will make cooking easier and tastier!

- If you have time, using dry beans is a very convenient and inexpensive solution, but there's a tiny thing to note. When you cook dry beans, you might notice that they're still pretty hard even after cooking them for hours. That probably means the beans are too old. If that is the case, unfortunately they won't get more tender as they cook, and there's not much you can do to salvage them.

- If you opt to use already-cooked beans, I recommend going for jarred beans over canned beans, because ultimately, they taste better, and I find they also have a better consistency.

- Whenever canned/jarred beans are mentioned in the cookbook, they are always with no salt, sugar or anything else added in—they are just beans and water.

- Try to buy as many organic and seasonal ingredients as possible; they taste so much better, and they are much better for the environment!

- To avoid food waste and buying vegetables out of season, try to pack your freezer with frozen veggies.

- Batch cooking is always a great idea! When trying recipes with longer cook times (recipes like Holiday Black Bean Nut Roast [page 28] and Classic Family Meat(less)loaf [page 24]), try doubling up the ingredient amounts, and freeze your leftovers into portions. This way, whenever you don't feel like cooking, you'll always have something delicious and nutritious waiting for you.

- All the recipes that require baking have been tested in the oven with the oven fan option off. If you'd like to use the fan option, remember to decrease the baking temperature by 40°F (20°C) for best results.

How to Prep and Cook Dried Beans

To make things easier, most of the recipes in this cookbook (unless specified) call for canned beans. I've written them this way because canned beans are so quick and convenient, and most of us usually have a few cans or jars stored in our cupboards at all times.

However, if you have a little extra time on hand, I always recommend buying dried beans and cooking them yourself. Dried beans are cheaper and have a much better flavor and texture when cooked. If you've never used dried beans before, don't let it intimidate you! The following steps explain how to prep and cook dried beans; the tips will work well with most legumes. The most important thing to remember is that there's no strict timeline when it comes to cooking beans. Even if you're using the same variety on two different occasions, you'll notice that the cooking time will change depending on the beans' age and where exactly they came from. Luckily, if you follow these steps, you'll be able to make a batch of perfectly cooked beans every single week.

1. PICK THE BEANS

Some supermarkets sell dry beans in bulk, which makes it easier to pick the best-looking ones. If you're buying prepackaged dry beans, have a good look through the package; if you see that they look old, shriveled and discolored, pick another bag.

2. SOAK THE BEANS

I highly recommend soaking dried beans first. Rinse them well under cool running water, then place them in a large bowl and add water to cover them by at least 3 inches (8 cm). Discard any beans that float to the surface. Leave the beans to soak for 8 hours on the counter; then you can proceed to cook them or let them soak for an extra 6 hours in the refrigerator. After they have finished soaking, give them a good rinse under cool running water and drain them. Now, they're ready to be cooked.

3. COOK THE BEANS

Transfer the beans into a large pot, and add water to cover them by at least 2 inches (5 cm). Bring them to a boil, then reduce the heat and let them simmer undisturbed for an hour. After this time, you can start checking if they're done. Most of the beans will take anywhere from 1 hour to 3 hours to cook through—this will depend on the type and size of the bean and how old they are.

Season the beans with sea salt when they're tender enough to bite through but still not completely cooked through. This will be anywhere from halfway to three-fourths of the way through cooking time.

For additional flavor, add a bay leaf, a carrot, a celery stick and an onion to the pot with the beans; remove them halfway through cooking and discard.

4. SAVE THE BEANS WITH OR WITHOUT THEIR COOKING WATER

Once the beans are cooked through, you can decide to store them with or without their cooking water. Storing the cooked beans in the water in which they have been cooking keeps them moist, adds extra nutritional value and keeps them more flavorful. Cooked beans stored in their cooking water are great for soups, chilis and mashes. Alternatively, you can drain the beans and use them for salads, sandwiches and taco fillings.

5. STORE THE COOKED BEANS

Once cooked, store the beans in an airtight container; they will keep well in the fridge for up to 4 days. You can also freeze them in a freezer-friendly container and store them in the freezer for up to 1 month. When you're ready to reheat your beans, you can use a little of their stored cooking liquid to enhance their flavor, or drain and rinse them for a more subtle flavor. (This is recommended if you're using the beans to prepare salads or one of the recipes in the dessert section of the book.)

Nutritious Mains with the Mighty Bean

There are so many ways to use beans to make a nutritious meal. Tiny but mighty, beans are a fantastic plant-based protein source. They're also super cheap and can easily become the star ingredient in your main course. What's more, they're incredibly versatile. Heat them on the stove with rice, roast them with seasonal veggies, stuff them into tacos or bake them into a hearty vegan pot pie. Your options are endless, and this chapter is a great place to start if you're looking for some inspiration.

You'll find plenty of delicious ways to enjoy beans as a main course, from a Classic Family Meat(less)loaf (page 24), The Ultimate Vegan Shepherd's Pie (page 15) and the Egg-Free Chickpea Frittata (page 19) to something a little more special, such as the Holiday Black Bean Nut Roast (page 28), which will make holiday cooking even more fun and tasty!

So, keep a couple of cans or bags of legumes in your pantry, and you'll be just a few minutes away from a delicious and fulfilling meal.

The Ultimate Vegan Shepherd's Pie

SERVINGS: 4

28 oz (800 g) russet or Yukon Gold potatoes, about 7–8 medium potatoes

3 tbsp (45 g) vegan butter

¼ cup (60 ml) rice milk, warmed

1 tsp fresh thyme leaves

A pinch of ground nutmeg

Sea salt and freshly cracked black pepper, to taste

2 tbsp (30 ml) extra-virgin olive oil

1 medium yellow onion, finely chopped

1 carrot, finely cubed

1 celery stalk, finely cubed

1 (15.5-oz [440-g]) can red kidney beans, rinsed and drained

1 (15.5-oz [440-g]) can black beans, rinsed and drained

1 tbsp (15 ml) vegan Worcestershire sauce

3 sprigs fresh thyme

1 tbsp (15 g) tomato paste

1 cup (240 ml) vegetable stock, warmed

Cooking Tip:

To speed up the recipe, you can prepare the mashed potatoes in advance, then warm them up before spreading them on top of the filling.

The perfect comforting family meal, this vegan version of classic British shepherd's pie features a layer of flavorful and healthy beans and veggies topped with fluffy mashed potatoes.

Place the potatoes in a large pot, cover them with lightly salted cold water and bring them to a boil. Simmer for about 20 minutes, or until the potatoes are tender and cooked through.

Once the potatoes are ready, drain them in a colander and peel them while hot.

Transfer the potatoes to a large bowl, add in the vegan butter and mash with a potato masher.

Slowly pour the milk into the bowl, and continue to mash the potatoes until the desired texture is reached.

Season the mashed potatoes with fresh thyme leaves, nutmeg, sea salt and freshly cracked black pepper to taste, then set aside.

Preheat the oven to 360°F (180°C), and arrange the baking rack in the middle shelf of the oven.

Heat a 10-inch (25-cm) oven-friendly skillet with olive oil over low heat. Add in the onion, carrot and celery and cook. Stir often for about 5 minutes, until the veggies have softened.

Add in the red kidney beans and black beans, then pour in the Worcestershire sauce, followed by the thyme sprigs and tomato paste. Stir the ingredients together for 2 minutes.

Pour the stock into the pot, bring to a gentle boil and simmer all the ingredients for 10 minutes. Discard the thyme sprigs and season the stock with additional sea salt and freshly cracked black pepper to taste.

Remove the skillet with the filling from the heat, and spread the prepared mashed potatoes over the filling, then ruffle the top with a fork. Alternatively, transfer the mashed potatoes into a piping bag and pipe it on top of the filling.

Transfer the skillet into the oven and bake the pie for 10 minutes, until the top is golden, then place under the broiler for an additional 5 minutes. Remove the pie from the oven, and allow it to rest for 5 minutes before serving.

Black Bean and Walnut Tacos to Share

1 tbsp (15 ml) vegetable or light olive oil

1⅔ cups (180 g) raw walnuts

1 tsp ground cumin

¼ tsp cayenne pepper

¼ tsp ground sweet paprika

¼ tsp garlic powder

1 tbsp (15 ml) walnut oil

1 tsp low-sodium soy sauce or tamari

1 cup (170 g) cooked black beans

TOMATO SALSA

4 large tomatoes, finely diced

½ medium red onion, finely minced

1 jalapeño, seeded and finely minced (optional)

1 tbsp (1 g) cilantro leaves, finely chopped

Juice of 1 lime

Sea salt and freshly cracked black pepper, to taste

TO SERVE

4 tortillas

1 avocado, mashed

4 tbsp (60 ml) vegan sour cream

1 tbsp (1 g) cilantro leaves, finely chopped

1 lime, cut into 4 wedges

Taco night with friends is the best, am I right? These plant-based tacos are loaded with flavor, because meat-free doesn't mean bland! Combine pantry staples such as nutrient-rich black beans, walnuts and spices, and in less than twenty minutes you'll have a meat-free filling that you can use for anything from stuffing tacos to quesadillas, or you can just serve it in a bowl with plenty of veggies.

Preheat the oven to 360°F (180°C), and arrange the baking rack in the middle shelf of the oven. Brush a baking tray with olive oil and set it aside.

Place the walnuts, cumin, cayenne pepper, paprika, garlic powder and walnut oil in a food processor and pulse until coarsely crumbled. Add the soy sauce and black beans and pulse again until you reach a crumbled texture. (It should resemble the texture of minced meat.)

Transfer the walnut mixture onto the prepared baking tray, and spread it out in an even layer. Bake for 15 minutes, until slightly browned and fragrant, stirring the mixture halfway through, then remove it from the oven and allow it to cool slightly.

In the meantime, prepare the tomato salsa. Place all the ingredients in a bowl and mix until combined, then season with a generous pinch of sea salt and freshly cracked black pepper to taste.

Arrange the tortillas on a large serving plate or board and top each tortilla with a few tablespoons (45 g) of the prepared walnut filling. Add a dollop of mashed avocado and vegan sour cream to each. Garnish with cilantro and serve with a lime wedge on the side.

> **Cooking Tip:** *You can prepare the walnut filling in advance and store it in an airtight container in the fridge for up to 3 days.*

Egg-Free Chickpea Frittata

10 oz (300 ml) cold water

2½ cups (230 g) chickpea flour

½ tsp turmeric powder

½ tsp garlic powder

4 tbsp (60 ml) extra-virgin olive oil, divided

¾ tsp sea salt, divided

Freshly cracked black pepper

1 onion, finely chopped

4–5 small broccoli florets, finely chopped

1 red bell pepper, finely chopped

6–7 cremini or shiitake mushrooms, chopped

Handful of fresh baby spinach leaves

The first bite of this super nutritious chickpea frittata will leave you totally impressed. It has a similar texture and taste to a classic frittata, but no eggs or cheese are involved! Feel free to substitute the veggies I used with your favorite ones, and try this hearty and nutritious chickpea frittata for breakfast, lunch or dinner—you won't be disappointed.

Place the water in a large bowl and slowly whisk in the flour until it's fully incorporated. Sprinkle the turmeric and garlic powder over the mixture, then whisk in 1 tablespoon (15 ml) of olive oil and season with ½ teaspoon of the sea salt, and add black pepper to taste. Whisk gently until the batter has reached a lump-free, velvety consistency. Cover the bowl and refrigerate it for 15 minutes.

Preheat the oven to 360°F (180°C), and arrange the baking tray onto the middle shelf of the oven.

Heat 2 tablespoons (30 ml) of olive oil in a large frying pan over medium heat, then add in the onion, broccoli, red bell pepper and mushrooms. Stir-fry them for about 5 minutes, pour in a splash of warm water, cover the pan with a lid and cook the vegetables for an additional 2 minutes. Add in the spinach leaves, cover again with a lid and continue to cook until the leaves have softened, about 2 minutes. Season with the remaining ¼ teaspoon of sea salt, and add black pepper to taste.

Grease a 9-inch (23-cm) springform cake pan with the remaining 1 tablespoon (15 ml) of olive oil, then distribute the veggies evenly over the surface of the pan. Pour in the prepared chickpea mixture, making sure to evenly cover the veggies, and bake it in the oven for 30 to 40 minutes, or until the frittata is cooked through. If the surface starts to brown too much, cover it with foil.

Remove the pan from the oven, allow the frittata to cool slightly, then transfer it onto a serving plate.

> **Cooking Tip:** *This frittata can easily be made ahead of time. In fact, it tastes even better the next day!*

Spicy Chickpea Shakshuka

2 (14-oz [400-g]) cans whole plum tomatoes

2 tbsp (30 ml) extra-virgin olive oil

½ medium red onion, finely chopped

1 red bell pepper, cut into strips

2 cloves of garlic, finely minced

1 tsp smoked paprika

½ tsp ground cumin

1 tsp red chili flakes

1 (15.5-oz [440-g]) can chickpeas, drained

Fine sea salt and freshly cracked black pepper, to taste

3 fresh basil leaves

1 tbsp (4 g) fresh parsley leaves, chopped, for topping

2 tbsp (30 ml) vegan sour cream, for topping (optional)

TO SERVE

4–5 slices of crusty bread, grilled

Shakshuka—a popular egg-based Middle Eastern dish—gets a vegan makeover by using chickpeas instead of eggs. This is a versatile and protein-rich dish that is great for breakfast, lunch or dinner. To make the most of it, choose your tomatoes wisely. I opt for whole peeled San Marzano tomatoes whenever possible, but crushed fire-roasted tomatoes work amazingly well too.

Transfer the tomatoes to a large bowl, and reserve their juices for later use. Gently crush the tomatoes with the back of a wooden spoon and set them aside.

Heat the olive oil in a large skillet over medium heat. Add the onion and bell pepper, and cook for 5 minutes, stirring occasionally, until they have softened and slightly browned.

Add the garlic, paprika, cumin and chili flakes; stir until fragrant, or for about 30 seconds.

Add the tomatoes into the skillet and stir to combine. Reduce the heat to a gentle simmer, and cook for about 15 minutes, adding the chickpeas halfway through the cooking time. If the mixture gets too dry, pour in up to ½ cup (120 ml) of the reserved tomato juice, then season with ½ teaspoon (or to taste) of fine sea salt, and add freshly cracked black pepper to taste. Stir in the fresh basil.

Remove the skillet from the heat and top with parsley and sour cream. Divide among four bowls and serve with crusty bread on the side.

> Cooking Tip: *Don't feel like having chickpeas today? No problem! This recipe works well with white beans too.*

Mushroom, Leek and White Bean Pie

3 tbsp (45 ml) extra-virgin olive oil (or vegan butter)

½ medium onion, finely sliced

2 garlic cloves, minced

2 leeks, white part only, finely sliced

1 lb (450 g) fresh mixed mushrooms (such as cremini, shiitake or porcini), stemmed and sliced

1 tsp fresh thyme leaves

A generous pinch of ground nutmeg

1 (15.5-oz [440-g]) can butter beans, rinsed and drained

2 tbsp (15 g) all-purpose flour

1 tbsp (15 ml) low-sodium soy sauce

2 cups (480 ml) vegetable stock, warmed

¼ tsp sea salt

1 (11-oz [320-g]) roll vegan puff pastry

1 tbsp (15 ml) nondairy milk (such as soy, oat or almond)

A vegan twist on a comfort food classic! This wintery, comforting and nutrient-packed butter bean, mushroom and leek pie is simple to make and delivers a fantastic family meal even carnivores will enjoy.

Preheat the oven to 360°F (180°C), and arrange the baking rack onto the middle shelf.

Heat the olive oil in a large skillet over medium-low heat. Add the onion, garlic, leeks and mushrooms. Cook the ingredients, stirring frequently for about 8 minutes, until veggies are slightly browned, adding a splash of warm water if the vegetables begin to brown too much. Add the thyme, followed by the nutmeg and butter beans, then sprinkle the mixture with flour and stir until the vegetables are coated.

Reduce the heat to low and add in the soy sauce and vegetable stock. Then season with the sea salt and cook, stirring frequently, for an additional 5 minutes, or until the stock thickens into a sauce. Pour the mixture into a 9-inch (23-cm) cast-iron pan or a 9-inch (23-cm) pie pan.

Remove the puff pastry dough from the refrigerator and drape it over the pan with the filling, removing the excess dough around the edges. Lightly crimp the edges with a fork and cut four small slits over the center to allow the steam to escape while baking the pie.

In a small bowl, mix together 1 teaspoon of water with the nondairy milk and lightly brush it over the surface of the dough.

Transfer the pie to the oven and bake for about 20 minutes, or until the top is golden and crispy, then remove from the oven. Allow the pie to cool for 5 to 7 minutes in the pan, and serve.

> **Cooking Tip:** *Play around with the veggies! Pumpkin, sweet potatoes, peas and broccoli would also work amazingly well in this awesome pie.*

Classic Family Meat(less)loaf

2 tbsp (30 ml) extra-virgin olive oil

1 medium yellow onion, minced

2 cups (150 g) shiitake mushrooms, finely sliced

1 garlic clove, minced

1 tsp fresh thyme leaves

Sea salt and freshly cracked black pepper, to taste

2 cups (200 g) unsalted roasted pecans

1 tbsp (15 g) tomato paste

1 tsp vegan Worcestershire sauce

1 medium sweet potato, peeled, steamed and chopped

5 oz (140 g) cooked black beans, rinsed and drained

5 oz (140 g) cooked pinto beans, rinsed and drained

½ cup (30 g) panko breadcrumbs

½ cup (120 ml) ketchup

Loaded with nutritious pinto and black beans and umami-rich sautéed veggies, this meatless meatloaf makes a delicious vegan alternative for a Sunday family meal or special occasion.

Preheat the oven to 360°F (180°C), and arrange the baking rack onto the middle shelf.

Heat the olive oil in a medium skillet over medium heat. Stir in the onion, mushrooms, garlic and thyme. Sauté all the ingredients for about 5 to 8 minutes, until slightly browned, stirring occasionally and adding a splash of water if the vegetables begin to brown too much. Adjust the seasoning by adding a generous pinch of sea salt and black pepper according to taste.

Remove the skillet from the heat and transfer the sautéed vegetables into the bowl of a food processor. Add in the pecans, tomato paste and Worcestershire sauce, and pulse briefly to combine. Add in the sweet potato, black beans and pinto beans and pulse all the ingredients together for about 5 to 10 seconds, or until crumbly but not pureed.

Transfer the mixture into a large bowl, add the breadcrumbs and slowly mix all the ingredients until you reach a dough-like consistency, adding a little extra breadcrumbs if necessary.

Transfer the mixture into a 10-inch x 5-inch (25-cm x 13-cm) loaf tin covered with parchment paper and press the surface down with a spoon to compact the meatloaf mixture. Brush the surface with the ketchup.

Cover the loaf tin with foil and bake in the oven for 30 minutes. Remove the foil and continue to bake for an additional 15 minutes, or until the surface is nicely golden brown.

Remove the loaf tin from the oven and allow it to cool for 10 minutes. Then transfer the loaf onto a serving plate or chopping board, slice it and serve.

> Cooking Tip: *For a gluten-free version, substitute the panko breadcrumbs with gluten-free breadcrumbs or coarsely ground gluten-free rolled oats.*

Broad Bean and Pea Risotto

4 cups (960 ml) vegetable stock, warmed

7 oz (200 g) fresh or frozen peas

5 oz (140 g) fresh or frozen broad beans, shelled

2 tbsp (30 ml) extra-virgin olive oil

1 shallot, finely minced

2 tbsp (30 g) vegan butter, divided

1 tsp fresh thyme leaves

¼ tsp sea salt, plus more to taste

Black pepper, to taste

10½ oz (300 g) Vialone Nano or Carnaroli rice

¼ cup (60 ml) dry vegan white wine

Juice of ½ lemon

Zest of 1 lemon, divided

1 tbsp (15 g) vegan Parmesan-style cheese, grated

This luxurious yet extremely easy broad bean and pea risotto is delicate but incredibly aromatic and secretly loaded with plant-based protein. It's one of those pretty and nutritious vegan meals that is simply perfect for celebrating the spring season.

Place the stock in a small pot and bring it to a gentle boil. Add the peas and broad beans into the boiling stock and cook for 4 minutes. Turn the heat off, remove the broad beans and peas with a slotted spoon and place them into a bowl; set them aside. Cover the pot with a lid to keep the stock warm.

Heat a skillet with the olive oil over medium-high heat, then add in the shallot and sauté it gently until it's soft, about 2 minutes. Transfer the blanched vegetables into the pan with the sweated shallot. Add in ½ tablespoon (7 g) of vegan butter and the thyme, and sauté the vegetables for an additional 2 minutes, then season with salt and pepper to taste and remove from the heat.

Transfer two-thirds of the vegetables to a blender, add one ladle of warm stock and blend until smooth, then set the pureed vegetables aside.

Heat ½ tablespoon (7 g) of vegan butter in a large pan over low heat, then add the rice. Toast it for 2 to 3 minutes, stirring continuously with a wooden spoon to avoid burning it, or until it has turned translucent. Add the wine, turn up the heat to medium-high and allow it to evaporate. Return the heat to medium-low, add the lemon juice, half of the lemon zest and one ladle of stock, and allow the rice to absorb it, then season with ¼ teaspoon of sea salt. Continue to cook, gradually adding in all the stock, whisking constantly until the rice is soft but still has a bite, about 15 minutes. Fold both the sautéed and pureed vegetables into the pan toward the end of cooking time, and stir to combine all the ingredients.

Remove the risotto from the heat. Next, stir in the vegan cheese, the remaining vegan butter and the lemon zest, then shake the pan vigorously to combine all the ingredients. The risotto should reach a smooth and creamy consistency. Divide the risotto among plates and serve immediately.

Cooking Tip: *Stir the risotto with a whisk rather than a wooden spoon to reach a creamier consistency. I like to use a silicone whisk, but you can also use a metal whisk—just make sure to whisk gently to avoid scraping the pan.*

Holiday Black Bean Nut Roast

2 cups (290 g) unsalted roasted mixed nuts (such as almonds, hazelnuts, walnuts, pecans or cashews)

2 tbsp (30 ml) extra-virgin olive oil

1 medium onion, finely minced

1 celery stick, finely chopped

2 medium carrots, coarsely grated

1 cup (70 g) cremini mushrooms, finely chopped

1 garlic clove, minced

1 tsp fresh thyme leaves

Sea salt and freshly cracked black pepper, to taste

¼ cup (65 g) almond butter

8 oz (225 g) cooked black beans, rinsed and drained

½ cup (60 g) dried soft cranberries

Zest of 1 lemon

2 tbsp (30 ml) almond milk

2 tbsp (10 g) panko breadcrumbs

This super easy main is a nutrient powerhouse thanks to the protein-rich black beans and roasted nuts! Serve this delicious nut roast with a super simple gravy to make a showstopping vegan alternative for Christmas dinner or any other special occasion.

Preheat the oven to 400°F (200°C) and arrange the baking rack onto the middle shelf.

Transfer the mixed nuts into a food processor; pulse until they are finely crumbled but not fully ground.

Heat the olive oil in medium skillet over medium heat. Stir in the onion, celery, carrots, mushrooms, garlic and thyme. Sauté all the ingredients for about 5 to 8 minutes, until the veggies are slightly browned, stirring occasionally and adding a splash of water if the vegetables begin to brown too much. Adjust the seasoning by adding a pinch of sea salt and black pepper according to taste.

In the meantime, transfer the almond butter and black beans into a large bowl, and roughly mash them with the help of a fork or potato masher.

Remove the pan from the heat, and transfer the sautéed vegetables into the bowl with the black bean mixture. Add in the dried cranberries, lemon zest and ground mixed nuts. Mix all the ingredients together. Slowly pour in the milk and breadcrumbs. If the mixture is too runny, stir in a few extra breadcrumbs.

Transfer the mixture into a 10-inch x 5-inch (25-cm x 13-cm) loaf tin covered with parchment paper, and press the surface down with a spoon to compact the nut roast mixture.

Cover the loaf tin with foil and bake in the oven for 30 minutes. Remove the foil and continue to bake for an additional 20 minutes, or until the nut roast is nicely golden brown on top.

(continued)

Holiday Black Bean Nut Roast (Continued)

VEGAN GRAVY

2 tbsp (30 g) vegan butter

2 tbsp (20 g) whole wheat flour

3 cups (720 ml) vegetable stock

1 tbsp (15 ml) low-sodium soy sauce or tamari

1 tsp vegan Worcestershire sauce

A pinch of garlic powder

1 tsp fresh thyme leaves

Sea salt and freshly cracked black pepper, to taste

1 rosemary sprig (optional)

In the meantime, prepare the gravy. Place the butter into a medium saucepan and heat over medium-low heat. Stir in the flour, a little at a time, and whisk until the gravy forms a thick paste.

Slowly whisk in the stock a little at a time, followed by the soy sauce, Worcestershire sauce, garlic powder and thyme. Continue to whisk the mixture and allow it to simmer for about 10 minutes, or until the sauce reaches a nicely thick and rich texture. Adjust the seasoning by adding a pinch of sea salt and freshly cracked black pepper to taste.

Remove the loaf tin from the oven, allow it to cool slightly, then transfer onto a serving plate or chopping board. Drizzle the gravy on top, garnish with optional sprig of rosemary and serve.

> Cooking Tip: *For a gluten-free version, substitute the panko breadcrumbs with coarsely ground gluten-free rolled oats, the soy sauce with tamari and the whole wheat flour with an all-purpose gluten-free flour blend.*

Asian-Style Mixed Bean Lettuce Wraps

1 tbsp (15 ml) toasted sesame oil

1 garlic clove, minced

½ cup (60 g) raw unsalted walnuts

2 tbsp (10 g) sesame seeds

1 (15.5-oz [440-g]) can mixed beans (such as butter bean, chickpeas and black beans), rinsed and drained

1 green onion, finely sliced

1 tsp ground Chinese five spice

2 tbsp (30 ml) low sodium soy sauce or tamari

Sea salt and freshly cracked black pepper, to taste

2 tbsp (4 g) fresh cilantro leaves, chopped

8–10 butter lettuce or romaine lettuce leaves

2 medium carrots, finely chopped into matchsticks

1 cup (70 g) purple cabbage, finely sliced

1 tbsp (10 g) roasted unsalted peanuts, roughly chopped, to garnish

DRESSING

½ cup (130 g) creamy peanut butter

Juice of 1 lime

2 tbsp (30 ml) rice vinegar

2 tbsp (30 ml) low-sodium soy sauce or tamari

1 tsp maple syrup

1 tsp sriracha

A pinch of garlic powder

3 tbsp (45 ml) water

Loaded with vibrant Asian flavors, these umami-rich lettuce wraps are low in carbs but high in protein. All you need is a can of cheap and healthy mixed beans and some fresh veggies to deliver a delicious meal in less than twenty minutes.

Heat the oil in a medium skillet over medium heat. Stir in the garlic, walnuts, sesame seeds, mixed beans, green onion, Chinese five spice and soy sauce. Stir-fry all the ingredients for about 5 to 8 minutes, until the veggies are slightly browned, stirring occasionally. Adjust the seasoning by adding a pinch of sea salt and black pepper or more five spice according to taste.

Remove the pan from the heat, stir in the cilantro leaves, transfer the filling into a large bowl and allow it to cool.

In the meantime, prepare the dressing. Place the peanut butter, lime juice, rice vinegar, soy sauce, maple syrup, sriracha, garlic powder and water in a small jar, and whisk all the ingredients together until creamy and smooth.

Arrange the lettuce leaves on a large serving plate or board, top each lettuce leaf with 2 tablespoons (30 g) of the prepared walnut and bean filling, chopped carrot and purple cabbage. Drizzle the peanut dressing on top, garnish with chopped peanuts and serve.

*See photo on page 12.

> **Cooking Tip:** *For a more substantial meal, you can add 1 cup (185 g) of cooked grain (such as quinoa, couscous or bulgur) into the walnut and bean filling.*

Veggie Taco-Stuffed Sweet Potatoes

4 medium or large sweet potatoes

1 tbsp (15 ml) extra-virgin olive oil

½ red onion, minced

1 garlic clove, grated

1 bell pepper, finely cubed

1 (15.5-oz [440-g]) can black beans, rinsed and drained

½ cup (70 g) cooked corn

1 small red chili pepper, seeded and finely minced

1 tbsp plus 1 tsp (20 ml) fresh lime juice, divided

2 tbsp (2 g) fresh cilantro leaves, finely chopped, plus more for garnish (optional)

1 tsp ground cumin

A pinch of cayenne pepper

Sea salt and freshly cracked black pepper, to taste

1 avocado

4 tbsp (60 ml) vegan yogurt or sour cream, for topping

These stuffed sweet potatoes come together easily with just a handful of ingredients, including meaty black beans, which are incredibly nutritious and filling. If you're looking for a great low-carb option for your taco night, this is the one!

Preheat the oven to 400°F (200°C), and arrange the baking rack in the middle shelf of the oven.

Wash and pat dry the potatoes, then use a fork to poke small holes all around each potato. Arrange them on a baking tray lined with parchment paper and lightly brush them with the olive oil. Bake the potatoes for around 30 to 40 minutes, or until they're soft and cooked through.

Meanwhile, prepare the filling. In a large bowl, mix together the onion, garlic, bell pepper, black beans, corn, red chili pepper, 1 tablespoon (15 ml) of fresh lime juice and cilantro until combined. Season with cumin, cayenne pepper and a generous pinch of sea salt and freshly cracked black pepper.

In a small bowl, combine the flesh of the avocado with the remaining 1 teaspoon of lime juice. Season with a generous pinch of sea salt and freshly cracked black pepper to taste, and refrigerate it until needed.

Remove the potatoes from the oven and slice them in half lengthwise, making sure not to cut them all the way through. Divide the black bean mixture among the four potatoes, top them with mashed avocado and the yogurt or sour cream and optional extra cilantro leaves.

> **Cooking Tip:** *For a nutritional boost, add 1 cup (185 g) of cooked quinoa or whole grain rice into the black bean filling.*

Evergreen Rice and Beans

2 tbsp (30 ml) extra-virgin olive oil

1 onion, finely minced

3 garlic cloves, finely minced

1 tsp ground cumin

2 cups (400 g) uncooked white long grain, basmati or jasmine rice

2 (15.5-oz [440-g]) cans black beans, rinsed and drained

4 cups (960 ml) vegetable stock

Sea salt and freshly cracked black pepper, to taste

Zest and juice of 1 lime

1 green onion, finely sliced

2 tbsp (2 g) fresh cilantro leaves, chopped

This classic rice and beans meal is loaded with vibrant flavors, comes together in one pot and can be served with pretty much anything you fancy, as it works wonderfully both as a side dish and a main course.

Heat the olive oil in a large stockpot or Dutch oven over medium-low heat. Stir in the onion and sauté until translucent, about 4 minutes. Add the garlic and cumin into the pot, followed by the rice and beans, and stir-fry all the ingredients for about 1 minute.

Pour in the stock and bring to a boil, then cover with a lid, reduce the heat to medium-low and cook for about 20 minutes, or until the rice is tender, stirring the ingredients halfway through the cooking time. Adjust the seasoning by adding a generous pinch of sea salt and black pepper according to taste.

Remove the pot from the heat, drizzle the lime juice all over the rice, stir in the green onion, lime zest and cilantro leaves and serve.

> **Cooking Tip:** *For a little heat, add a generous pinch of cayenne pepper or a finely minced red chili pepper right after adding the ground cumin into the pot.*

My Go-To Moong Dal Omelet

¾ cup (140 g) moong dal (split mung beans)

3 cups (720 ml) water, lukewarm

¼ tsp garlic powder

½ tsp onion powder

¼ tsp ground turmeric

A pinch of smoked paprika

1 tsp baking powder

1½ tsp (10 g) sea salt or kala namak (Indian black salt)

A pinch of freshly cracked black pepper

1 cup (240 ml) canned light coconut milk

2 tbsp (30 ml) extra-virgin olive oil or vegan butter

TO SERVE

Vegetables of your choice (such as avocado, mushroom, spinach, tomatoes and baby salad leaves)

Vegan cheese

1 tbsp (1 g) fresh parsley leaves, chopped

This vegan omelet, also nicknamed "Moonglet," is made with moong dal, which are split and skinned green mung beans. They have a lovely nutty flavor (slightly milder than chickpea flour) and make a great option for delicious egg-free omelets!

Rinse and place the moong dal in a large bowl and cover with at least 3 cups (720 ml) of lukewarm water. Cover the bowl and let it rest for 3 hours or overnight.

Drain the moong dal and transfer them to a blender. Add in the garlic powder, onion powder, turmeric, paprika, baking powder, sea salt, black pepper and coconut milk. Blend for 10 seconds, or until you get a creamy lump-free batter; the mixture should be smooth and fluffy and not too runny. If it's too dry, add an extra 2 to 3 tablespoons (30 to 45 ml) of coconut milk and blend to combine.

Brush a medium nonstick skillet with the olive oil and place it over medium heat. Pour about a ladle of omelet batter into the skillet, and spread it to almost reach the edges of the pan.

Cover the skillet with a lid and cook the omelet for about 2 minutes, or until the edges are dry and the center is just about set. Loosen the bottom of the omelet with a spatula and flip it onto the other side. Continue to cook it for another minute, until golden on both sides, then transfer onto a serving plate. Repeat the process with the remaining batter, until all the batter has been used up. Fill the omelets with your favorite vegetables and/or vegan cheese, garnish with parsley and serve.

Butter Bean Ratatouille

4 tbsp (60 ml) extra-virgin olive oil, divided

½ large red or yellow onion, finely chopped

1 garlic clove, minced

1 red bell pepper, finely chopped

1 (14-oz [400-g]) can whole plum tomatoes

1 tsp brown sugar

1 tbsp (15 ml) balsamic vinegar

1 tsp dried oregano, plus more for sprinkling

1 tsp fresh thyme leaves

Sea salt and freshly cracked black pepper, to taste

2 medium zucchini, cubed

1 large eggplant, cubed

3–4 fresh basil leaves

1 (15.5-oz [440-g]) can butter beans, rinsed and drained

2 thyme sprigs

Cooking Tip:

To make things easier, I recommend using a Dutch oven, but you can use a regular large skillet, then transfer the ratatouille to an oven-proof baking dish before baking in a conventional oven.

Here, seasonal veggies are slow-cooked together to make a dish that truly celebrates summer flavors. Butter beans give a most-welcome protein boost, turning this classic French side dish into a proper meal. Whether you serve it with crusty sourdough bread or as a glorious filling for a baked potato, this easy ratatouille is sure to make a satisfying veggie-loaded lunch or dinner option.

Heat 2 tablespoons (30 ml) of olive oil in a medium-large Dutch oven over medium-low heat. Add in the onion and garlic, followed by the red bell pepper, tomatoes and their juices.

Cook all the vegetables for 5 minutes, then stir in the brown sugar, balsamic vinegar, oregano and thyme. Mix all the ingredients together, and gently crush the tomatoes with the back of a wooden spoon.

Simmer all the ingredients over medium-low heat for about 15 minutes, until the sauce is slightly sweetened, stirring occasionally, then season with ¼ teaspoon (or to taste) of fine sea salt and add freshly cracked black pepper to taste.

Transfer the prepared sauce into a food processor and blend it until creamy but still a bit chunky. Add a splash of hot water if necessary, then set the sauce aside until needed.

Preheat the oven to 425°F (210°C), and arrange the baking rack onto the middle shelf of the oven.

Return the pot to the stove, and heat 1 tablespoon (15 ml) of olive oil over medium-low heat. Add the zucchini and eggplant and stir-fry them for 5 minutes, until they're slightly softened. Stir in the prepared tomato sauce, followed by the basil.

Season the vegetables with a pinch of extra oregano, sea salt and black pepper on top, and finish off with the remaining 1 tablespoon (15 ml) of olive oil.

Bake the ratatouille for about 20 to 30 minutes in the oven, stirring the butter beans in halfway through the cooking time. Continue to cook until the vegetables are tender and the sauce is softly bubbling.

Remove the pot from the oven, allow the ratatouille to cool for 5 minutes, top with the thyme sprigs then serve.

Plant-Based Burgers That Won't Make You Miss Meat

I've been really into plant-based burgers for the past few years, so it was an absolute no-brainer to include a chapter dedicated to this iconic American dish.

There's no need to buy premade and fat-loaded supermarket vegan burgers when you can sit down to one of the healthy and tasty bean burger recipes in this chapter! From The Ultimate Black Bean Burger (page 43) and Quinoa and White Bean Burger with Spicy Avocado Cream (page 47) to the Green Veggie Chickpea Burger (page 51), there's a choice for pretty much any occasion and taste. Making your own burgers means you know exactly what's inside, plus they're quick to make, loaded with nutritious ingredients and, best of all, they're absolutely *packed* with flavor. These meatless bean burgers don't require any complicated steps, are perfect for making ahead and will make both the meat eaters and non-meat eaters in your life happy! Make sure to serve all these recipes with fries and your choice of side dishes, creamy sauces and colorful salads.

So if you're looking for new burger recipes for your summer feast or weekend dinner treat, look no further. These plant-based burgers have it all!

The Ultimate Black Bean Burger

2 (15.5-oz [440-g]) cans black beans, rinsed and drained

1 tbsp (15 ml) low-sodium soy sauce or tamari

½ onion, finely minced

2 garlic cloves, grated

1 tsp cayenne pepper

1 tsp smoked paprika

1 tbsp (10 g) sesame seeds

A pinch of freshly cracked black pepper

1⅓ cup (75 g) panko breadcrumbs

2 tbsp (30 ml) extra-virgin olive or vegetable oil, for frying

TO SERVE

4-6 burger buns

Vegetables of choice for toppings (such as tomatoes, lettuce leaves, onion and avocado)

Black bean burgers have taken the internet by the storm in the past few years and for all the right reasons! They're super cheap, easy to make and taste just as good, if not better, than meat burgers. This is my ultimate black bean burger recipe—it's packed with high-protein beans and tons of flavorful spices, and it comes together with the most simple and low cost pantry-friendly ingredients.

Pour the black beans into a large bowl, then add the soy sauce, onion, garlic, cayenne pepper, paprika, sesame seeds, black pepper and breadcrumbs. Mix to combine all the ingredients, mashing them with a potato masher but leaving some of the beans whole for added texture.

Use your hands or an ice cream scoop to form four large or six smaller patties. If the mixture is too wet, add an extra tablespoon (4 g) of breadcrumbs. If it's too dry, add a tablespoon (15 ml) of water. Arrange the patties onto a baking tray covered with parchment paper, and put them in the refrigerator to set for 30 minutes.

Brush a large skillet with the olive oil, and heat it over medium heat. Add the patties and cook them for 4 minutes on each side, until they're crispy and golden brown.

Remove the patties from the skillet, and serve them with your preferred burger buns and toppings.

Cooking Tip: *Leftover patties can be stored in the refrigerator for up to 2 days and in the freezer up to 1 month. Reheat them in the oven for 5 minutes (or 15 minutes if they're frozen) before serving them.*

Spicy Chickpea Burger with Tzatziki

2 (15.5-oz [440-g]) cans chickpeas, rinsed and drained

½ red onion, finely minced

2 garlic cloves, grated

1 tsp smoked paprika

1 tbsp (2 g) fresh parsley leaves, finely chopped

1 tsp lemon zest

A pinch of freshly cracked black pepper

1⅓ cup (75 g) panko breadcrumbs

2 tbsp (30 ml) olive or vegetable oil, for frying

TZATZIKI SAUCE

1 cucumber, peeled and finely shredded

1 cup (240 ml) plain soy yogurt

1 garlic clove, grated

1 tbsp (1 g) fresh mint leaves, finely chopped

1 tbsp (15 ml) extra-virgin olive oil

1 tbsp (15 ml) fresh lemon juice

Sea salt and freshly cracked black pepper, to taste

TO SERVE

4 lettuce leaves

1 tomato, sliced

4 burger buns

This Greek-inspired burger is packed with delicious and nutrient-rich chickpeas and served with a mouthwatering tzatziki sauce—perfect for a summer feast!

Place the chickpeas in a large bowl, followed by the onion, garlic, paprika, parsley, lemon zest, black pepper and breadcrumbs. Mix to combine all the ingredients, mashing them with a potato masher but leaving some of the chickpeas whole for added texture.

Use your hands or an ice cream scoop to form four patties. If the mixture is too wet, add an extra tablespoon (4 g) of breadcrumbs. If it's too dry, add a tablespoon (15 ml) of water. Arrange the patties on a baking tray covered with parchment paper, and put them in the refrigerator to set for 30 minutes.

For the tzatziki sauce, start by placing the shredded cucumber on paper towels and pat it dry to absorb as much moisture as possible. Transfer the cucumber to a bowl, then add the yogurt, garlic, mint, olive oil and lemon juice. Season the sauce with ¼ tsp of sea salt (or to taste), and add freshly cracked black pepper, then refrigerate until the burgers are ready to serve.

Brush a large skillet with the olive oil and heat it over medium heat, then add the patties and cook them for 4 minutes on each side, until crispy and golden brown.

Remove the patties from the skillet and assemble your burgers. Layer 1 lettuce leaf, 1 slice of tomato, 1 burger and a generous dollop of the prepared tzatziki sauce over the base of each bun, top with the other half of the bun and serve.

> Cooking Tip: *Leftover patties can be stored in the refrigerator for up to 2 days and in the freezer up to 1 month. Reheat them in the oven for 5 minutes (or 15 minutes if they're frozen) before serving them.*

Quinoa and White Bean Burger with Spicy Avocado Cream

SERVINGS: 4–6

3 tbsp (30 g) flaxseeds, ground

⅓ cup (80 ml) water, warmed

½ cup (90 g) cooked quinoa

1 (15.5-oz [440-g]) can butter beans, rinsed and drained

½ red onion, finely minced

2 garlic cloves, grated

¼ tsp ground cumin

1 tbsp (1 g) fresh cilantro leaves, finely chopped

1 tsp lemon zest

Sea salt and black pepper, to taste

½ cup (30 g) panko breadcrumbs

2 tbsp (30 ml) olive or vegetable oil, for frying

SPICY AVOCADO CREAM

1 large avocado, chopped

2 tbsp (30 ml) plain soy yogurt

1 garlic clove, grated

1 tbsp (1 g) fresh cilantro leaves, finely chopped

½ red chili pepper, seeded and minced

1 tbsp (15 ml) fresh lemon juice

Sea salt and freshly cracked black pepper, to taste

TO SERVE

4 lettuce leaves

1 tomato, sliced

4 burger buns

These protein-packed quinoa and bean burgers are the perfect example of how homemade burgers can be absolutely delicious, full of flavor and loaded with oh-so-good-for-you ingredients—all at the same time! Serve them with a spicy avocado cream for a nice fiery kick!

Place the flaxseeds and water in a small bowl, whisk them together, then let them sit for 5 minutes or until thickened.

Place the quinoa and beans into a large bowl, and mash them with a potato masher until they reach a chunky consistency. Add in the onion, garlic, cumin, cilantro, lemon zest, black pepper, breadcrumbs and the flaxseed mixture. Mix to combine all the ingredients, then season with ¼ teaspoon (or to taste) of sea salt and freshly cracked black pepper to taste.

Use your hands or an ice cream scoop to form four patties. If the mixture is too wet, add an extra tablespoon (4 g) of panko breadcrumbs. If it's too dry, add a tablespoon (15 ml) of water. Arrange the patties onto a baking tray covered with parchment paper, and place them in the refrigerator to set for 30 minutes.

For the spicy avocado cream, transfer the avocado to a food processor, then add the yogurt, garlic, cilantro, red chili pepper and lemon juice, and blend all the ingredients until creamy. Season the cream with ¼ teaspoon of sea salt (or to taste), and add a pinch of freshly cracked black pepper, then refrigerate until the burgers are ready to serve.

Brush a large skillet with the olive oil and heat it over medium heat, then add the patties and cook them for 4 minutes on each side, until they're crispy and golden brown.

Remove the patties from the skillet and assemble your burgers. Layer 1 lettuce leaf, 1 slice of tomato, 1 burger and a dollop of the prepared avocado sauce over the base of each bun, top with the other half of the bun and serve.

> **Cooking Tip:** *Leftover patties can be stored in the refrigerator for up to 2 days and in the freezer up to 1 month. Reheat them in the oven for 5 minutes (or 15 minutes if they're frozen) before serving them.*

Veggie-Loaded Sweet Potato and Kidney Bean Burger

1 (15.5-oz [440-g]) can kidney beans, rinsed and drained

1 medium sweet potato, peeled, steamed and mashed

4–5 small broccoli florets, steamed

½ onion, finely minced

1 tsp garlic powder

1 tsp cayenne pepper

1 tsp smoked paprika

1 tsp ground cumin

¾ cup (70 g) gluten-free quick rolled oats or instant oats

½ tsp fine sea salt, or to taste

A pinch of freshly cracked black pepper

2 tbsp (30 ml) olive or vegetable oil, for frying

TO SERVE

4–6 burger buns

Vegetables of choice for toppings (such as tomatoes, lettuce leaves, onion and avocado)

This is the perfect burger for picky eaters who don't usually love their veggies. This nutritious bean burger has some extra healthy vegetables cleverly sneaked in, and it comes together in just about twenty minutes.

Place the kidney beans in a large bowl, and gently mash them with a masher, leaving some of the beans whole for added texture. Add in the mashed sweet potato and broccoli, followed by the onion, garlic, cayenne pepper, paprika, cumin, rolled oats and salt and black pepper. Mix to combine all the ingredients, then taste and adjust the seasoning.

Use your hands or an ice cream scoop to form four large or six smaller patties. If the mixture is too wet, add an extra tablespoon (6 g) of oats. If it's too dry, add a tablespoon (15 ml) of water. Arrange the patties onto a baking tray covered with parchment paper and put them in the refrigerator to set for 30 minutes.

Brush a large skillet with the olive oil and heat it over medium heat, then add the patties and cook them for 4 minutes on each side until they're crispy and golden brown.

Remove the patties from the skillet, and serve them with your preferred burger buns and toppings.

> Cooking Tip: *Leftover patties can be stored in the refrigerator for up to 2 days and in the freezer up to 1 month. Reheat them in the oven for 5 minutes (or 15 minutes if they're frozen) before serving them.*

Green Veggie Chickpea Burger

2 tbsp (20 g) flaxseeds, ground

¼ cup (60 ml) water, warmed

3 tbsp (45 ml) extra-virgin olive oil, divided

½ onion, minced

2 garlic cloves, minced

2 cups (180 g) broccoli florets, finely chopped

1 (15.5-oz [440-g]) can chickpeas, rinsed and drained

⅓ cup (45 g) frozen peas, thawed

½ cup (10 g) fresh parsley leaves

Zest of half lemon

A pinch of black pepper

¼ cup (20 g) nutritional yeast

¼ cup (15 g) panko breadcrumbs

GREEN GODDESS DRESSING

1 large avocado

2 tbsp (30 ml) extra-virgin olive oil

2 tbsp (30 ml) water

1 garlic clove, grated

¼ cup (15 g) fresh parsley leaves

¼ cup (10 g) chives, chopped

¼ cup (10 g) fresh basil leaves

Juice of half lemon

Sea salt and freshly cracked black pepper, to taste

TO SERVE

4 lettuce leaves

1 tomato, sliced

4 burger buns

These green chickpea burgers are loaded with flavor and nutrient-packed ingredients like flaxseeds, nutritional yeast, broccoli and peas. Once you have mastered the basics, play around with the spices to customize them, and don't forget the sauce—it's so good!

Place the flaxseeds and water in a small bowl, whisk them together and let them sit for 5 minutes or until thickened.

Heat 1 tablespoon (15 ml) of olive oil in a skillet over medium heat, add the onion and sauté until translucent, about 5 minutes, then add in the garlic and broccoli, and continue to cook the vegetables for 5 minutes, stirring often. Transfer the cooked vegetables to a food processor. Add the chickpeas, peas, parsley, lemon zest and a pinch of black pepper, and pulse to combine all the ingredients. Add in the nutritional yeast followed by the breadcrumbs and blend until reaching a thick texture, but not pureed.

Use your hands or an ice cream scoop to form four large patties. If the mixture is too wet, add an extra tablespoon (4 g) of panko. If it's too dry, add a tablespoon (15 ml) of water. Arrange the patties onto a baking tray covered with parchment paper and put them in the refrigerator to set for 30 minutes.

For the green goddess dressing, place all the ingredients into a food processor and blend until smooth, season with a generous pinch of sea salt and freshly cracked black pepper to taste, then taste and add a little more lemon juice for a more tangy flavor, if desired. Set the dressing aside until the burgers are ready to serve.

Brush a large skillet with the remaining olive oil, and heat it over medium heat, then add the patties and cook for 4 minutes on each side, until they're crispy and golden brown.

Remove the patties from the skillet and assemble your burgers. Layer 1 lettuce leaf, 1 slice of tomato, 1 burger and a dollop of the prepared dressing over the base of each bun, top with the other half of the bun and serve.

> **Cooking Tips:** *For a gluten-free burger, substitute the panko breadcrumbs with the same amount of gluten-free quick oats. Store leftover patties in the fridge for up to 2 days and in the freezer up to 1 month. Reheat them in the oven for 5 minutes (or 15 minutes if they're frozen) before serving.*

Next-Level Mushroom Bean Burger

4 tbsp (60 ml) extra-virgin olive oil, divided

½ yellow onion, minced

1 garlic clove, grated

1 cup (70 g) shiitake or cremini mushrooms, finely chopped

½ tsp ground cumin

Sea salt and freshly cracked black pepper

1 (15.5-oz [440-g]) can pinto beans, rinsed and drained

1 tbsp (2 g) fresh parsley leaves, finely chopped

⅔ cup (60 g) gluten-free quick oats

CARAMELIZED ONIONS

2 tbsp (30 ml) extra-virgin olive oil

3 medium yellow onions, finely sliced

1 tbsp (15 g) brown sugar

1 tbsp (15 ml) balsamic vinegar

A pinch of sea salt

TO SERVE

4 lettuce leaves

1 tomato, sliced

4 burger buns

This gluten-free mushroom burger is a healthier alternative to beef and will surprise your tastebuds! The umami-rich mushrooms and inexpensive protein-filled pinto beans add tons of flavor and texture. The caramelized onions bring this burger to the next level!

Heat 2 tablespoons (30 ml) of olive oil in a skillet over medium-low heat. Add in the onion, garlic, mushrooms and cumin and stir-fry them for 5 minutes, adding a splash of water if the vegetables begin to brown too much. Season with ¼ teaspoon (or to taste) of sea salt, and add freshly cracked black pepper to taste.

Place the pinto beans in a large bowl and mash them thoroughly with a potato masher. Alternatively, you can blend them in a food processor. Add in the mushroom mixture, then add the parsley and quick oats. Mix everything together and adjust the seasoning. If the mixture is too dry, add a splash of water. If it's too wet, add an extra tablespoon (6 g) of quick oats.

Use your hands or an ice cream scoop to form four patties. Arrange the patties on a baking tray covered with parchment paper, and put them in the refrigerator to set for 30 minutes.

For the caramelized onions, heat the olive oil in a medium skillet over low heat. Add the onions and allow them to cook for 15 minutes, stirring them often to prevent them from burning. Once they have softened, add in the sugar and balsamic vinegar and let them cook for an additional 10 minutes. Season them with a generous pinch of sea salt, then turn the heat off and set them aside until needed.

Brush a large skillet with the remaining 2 tablespoons (30 ml) of olive oil, and heat it over medium heat. Add the patties and cook them for 4 minutes on each side, until they're crispy and golden brown.

Remove the patties from the skillet and assemble your burgers. Layer 1 lettuce leaf, 1 slice of tomato, 1 burger and a generous dollop of caramelized onions over the base of each bun, top with the other half of the bun and serve.

> Cooking Tip: *Store the leftover patties in the fridge for up to 2 days and in the freezer for up to 1 month. Reheat them in the oven for 5 minutes (or 15 minutes if they're frozen) before serving them.*

Cozy and Comforting Soups, Curries and Chilis

Whether you're ditching meat entirely or looking to reduce your animal-product consumption and switch up your weekly meals, beans are there for you. Legumes are some of the best foods you can eat for fiber, protein, vitamins and minerals. Even better, their versatile flavor and texture allows you to create so many dishes with just a can of beans, especially when it comes to cold-weather cooking.

Hearty, comforting and filling, beans make perfect winter stews, soups and wholesome chilis. Made with cannellini beans, pinto beans, kidney beans, chickpeas and black-eyed peas, the recipes from this chapter are exactly what you need on a chilly day.

This is probably my favorite chapter, because there is so much flavor in these recipes. They require the most basic ingredients and minimum effort—perfect for when you crave a quick, nourishing meal after a cold day out. Try the quick Ten-Minute Chickpea Spinach Curry (page 66) for a last-minute fulfilling meal, or spice up your dinner menu with the classic Smoky and Spicy Chili Sin Carne (page 58), and for those days when you need a punch of flavor, make sure you give the Thai-Style Curry with Black-Eyed Peas (page 61) a shot!

Garlicky White Kidney Bean Soup

3 (15.5-oz [440-g]) cans white kidney beans, rinsed and drained, divided

4 cups (960 ml) vegetable stock, warmed, divided

3 tbsp (45 ml) extra-virgin olive oil, divided

1 medium-sized Yukon Gold potato, peeled and finely cubed

4 garlic cloves, minced

1 tsp fresh thyme leaves

2 cups (130 g) kale, chopped

Sea salt, to taste

1 tsp red chili pepper flakes (optional)

Freshly cracked black pepper, to taste

This easy, nutrient-rich white kidney bean soup can be whipped up with just a handful of ingredients, such as inexpensive and pantry-friendly canned beans, garlic and potatoes. Fresh thyme and garlic will give this humble dish a nice kick of flavor, and you can add some red chili for some extra heat. Serve it with crusty artisanal bread slices or croutons, and you can call it a meal!

Place one-third of the beans in a blender, pour in ½ cup (120 ml) of the stock and blend until smooth. Set the creamy beans aside until needed.

Heat 2 tablespoons (30 ml) of olive oil in a large pot over medium-low heat, add the potato and garlic and cook until they both begin to turn golden, adding a splash of warm water if they begin to brown too much.

Add in the remaining two-thirds of the beans and thyme; stir occasionally for 5 minutes.

Pour the creamed beans and the remaining vegetable stock into the pot, and simmer all the ingredients for 8 minutes, stirring occasionally. Add the kale to the pot, and continue to cook for an additional 2 minutes, then season with sea salt to taste and optional red chili pepper flakes.

Remove the pot from the heat, divide the soup into bowls, top with freshly cracked black pepper, drizzle with the remaining olive oil and serve.

> Cooking Tip: *White kidney beans (also called cannellini beans) work wonderfully here with their creamy texture and delicate nutty flavor. However, feel free to use any other kind of white beans: navy beans, baby lima beans and great northern beans will all work well.*

Smoky and Spicy Chili Sin Carne

3 tbsp (45 ml) extra-virgin olive oil

1 medium yellow onion, finely chopped

2 garlic cloves, minced

2 carrots, finely cubed

2 celery stalks, finely sliced

1 red bell pepper, seeded and cubed

1 (15.5-oz [440-g]) can black beans, rinsed and drained

1 (15.5-oz [440-g]) can pinto beans, rinsed and drained

1–2 tsp (1 g) red chili powder or flakes

¼ tsp cayenne pepper (or to taste)

1 tsp ground cumin

1 tsp dried oregano

1 tbsp (15 g) tomato paste

2 (14-oz [400-g]) cans crushed tomatoes

½ cup (120 ml) vegetable stock or water, warmed

Sea salt and freshly cracked black pepper, to taste

TO SERVE

1 tbsp (3 g) cilantro leaves, finely chopped

1 avocado, diced

1 lime, cut into 4 wedges

4 tbsp (60 ml) vegan sour cream

This vegan chili sin carne is the perfect winter comfort food. It is every bit as comforting, filling and flavorful as classic beef chili. I like to follow the traditional recipe and simply replace the meat with extra protein-boosted pinto and black beans—it's as simple as that! As an added bonus, this spicy and smoky chili makes a great option for meal prep for a busy week ahead, or when entertaining a large crowd.

Heat a medium stock pot or Dutch oven with the olive oil over low heat. Add in the onion, garlic, carrots, celery and red bell pepper and cook for about 5 minutes, stirring often, until the veggies have softened.

Add in the beans, followed by the spices, oregano and tomato paste; combine ingredients and stir continuously for 2 minutes.

Stir in the crushed tomatoes. Pour in the stock, then bring it to a gentle boil and simmer for 15 to 20 minutes. Season with ¼ teaspoon (or to taste) of sea salt and add freshly cracked black pepper to taste.

Divide the chili among bowls. Top each one with cilantro, avocado, lime and sour cream and serve.

> Cooking Tip: *This chili freezes beautifully! Make a double batch and freeze leftovers into portions to enjoy during the week.*

Thai-Style Curry with Black-Eyed Peas

2 tbsp (30 ml) extra-virgin olive oil

½ medium onion, finely sliced

1 garlic clove, minced

1 tsp fresh ginger, peeled and grated

1 red chili pepper, whole

½ lemongrass stalk

½ red bell pepper, finely sliced

1 carrot, sliced

1 bok choy, cut into quarters lengthwise

1 cup (60 g) snow peas

1 cup (90 g) small broccoli florets

2 cups (340 g) cooked black-eyed peas

2 tbsp (30 g) Thai red curry paste

1 tbsp (15 g) brown sugar

1 tsp dark soy sauce or tamari

1 can (13.5-oz [398-ml]) unsweetened coconut milk

1 tbsp (5 ml) fresh lime juice

TO SERVE

1⅔ cups (310 g) steamed jasmine or basmati rice

2 tbsp (2 g) fresh coriander leaves, minced, divided

1 lime, cut into wedges

Thai curry paste is a fantastic way to quickly add plenty of flavor into a dish, saving you lots of time and effort. This curry features tons of veggies and protein-loaded black-eyed peas for a well-balanced meal you can put together in an instant.

Heat the oil in a large pan or wok over medium heat, then add in the onion, garlic, ginger, red chili pepper and lemongrass, and stir-fry them for 2 minutes, until fragrant.

Add the bell pepper, carrot, bok choy, snow peas and broccoli, followed by the black-eyed peas, and stir-fry all the ingredients for 3 minutes, until they're slightly browned, adding a splash of water if they begin to brown too much.

Stir in the curry paste followed by the brown sugar and soy sauce, then pour the coconut milk into the pan. Allow all the ingredients to cook for 5 minutes.

Remove the lemongrass and whole chili pepper from the pan and turn the heat off.

Drizzle the curry with the lime juice and divide it into four bowls. Divide the steamed rice between the bowls, sprinkle ½ tablespoon of fresh coriander leaves on top of each bowl and serve with a lime wedge on the side.

Cooking Tip: *This curry works great with other beans too! Try pinto beans, mung beans or edamame for a different version.*

Easy Pumpkin Soup with Hidden Beans

2 tbsp (30 ml) extra-virgin olive oil

1 medium white onion, roughly chopped

2 pounds (900 g) pumpkin flesh, finely cubed

5 oz (140 g) cooked cannellini beans

1 tsp fresh thyme leaves

1 tsp fresh ginger, grated

Sea salt and freshly cracked black pepper, to taste

4 cups (960 ml) vegetable stock

TO SERVE

4–5 mushrooms, sautéed (optional)

Handful of croutons (optional)

1 tbsp (7 g) pumpkin seeds, toasted (optional)

1 tbsp (1 g) fresh parsley, chopped (optional)

This easy pumpkin soup is definitely one for the picky eaters! It's thick, velvety and so full of flavor. Best of all, you get a nice protein kick thanks to the addition of cannellini beans, which are blended in and hidden in the creamy soup. This dish freezes beautifully too, so you can easily make a big batch and store it in the freezer for up to two months, then thaw and reheat it using your chosen method.

Heat olive oil in a large pot over medium high heat. Add in the chopped onion, pumpkin and beans, followed by the thyme and ginger. Sauté the ingredients for 5 minutes, or until the vegetables begin to soften, then season with ½ teaspoon (or to taste) of sea salt and a generous pinch of freshly cracked black pepper.

Pour in the stock, then cover the pot with a lid and simmer for 10 to 15 minutes, or until the vegetables are cooked through.

Remove the pot from the heat and take 1 cup (240 ml) of stock out from the pot.

Transfer the soup into a blender or use an immersion blender to blend all the ingredients until they reach your desired consistency, adding in the reserved stock if necessary.

Divide the pumpkin soup among four bowls, season with more freshly cracked pepper, sautéed mushrooms, croutons, pumpkin seeds and parsley, if desired, and serve immediately.

Cooking Tips: *Use any type of edible pumpkin you like or butternut squash. To add some texture, feel free to leave some beans unblended and/or top the soup with warm crispy croutons.*

Hearty and Nourishing Minestrone

2 tbsp (30 ml) extra-virgin olive oil

1 medium yellow onion, finely cubed

1 small leek, finely sliced

2 celery stalks, cubed

2 carrots, cubed

1 large zucchini, cubed

1 large potato, peeled and cubed

1 can (15.5-oz [440-g]) borlotti beans, rinsed and drained

1 can (14-oz [400 g]) peeled plum tomatoes (preferably San Marzano tomatoes)

4 cups (960 ml) vegetable stock, warmed

1 tsp fine sea salt

Freshly cracked black pepper, to taste

1 cup (135 g) frozen peas

2 cups (60 g) baby spinach or baby kale

2 tbsp (2 g) fresh parsley leaves, chopped

A pinch of red chili flakes

4–5 slices of crusty bread, grilled (optional)

Colder nights call for hot soup bowls. This classic Italian minestrone boasts a whole array of veggies, a delicious tomato broth and protein-rich borlotti beans for the coziest dinner you could possibly make. Minestrone tastes even better the day after it's made, so prep it the night before for a comforting future lunch or dinner. For the best texture, make sure to cut your veggies into small, even chunks!

Heat the olive oil in a large stockpot or Dutch oven over medium-low heat. Add the onion, leek, celery, carrots, zucchini and potato, and sauté all the vegetables for about 5 minutes, stirring often.

Add in the beans, the tomatoes and their juice, followed by the stock. Season with 1 teaspoon of fine sea salt and add freshly cracked black pepper to taste. Stir to combine all the ingredients, cover the pot with a lid and bring it to a boil over medium-high heat.

Reduce the heat to medium-low, remove the lid and simmer the minestrone for about 30 minutes, or until the potatoes and carrots are tender.

Fold in the peas and spinach, and cook the minestrone for an additional 2 minutes. Taste the soup and season with additional sea salt and freshly cracked black pepper as needed.

Remove the pot from the heat and ladle the minestrone into the bowls. Top with chopped parsley and a pinch of chili flakes, and serve with crusty bread.

Cooking Tip: *Make this basic version your blank canvas and add more or fewer veggies according to your taste or the season—cauliflower, pumpkin, savoy cabbage and green beans are just a few options that would work wonderfully here.*

Ten-Minute Chickpea Spinach Curry

3 medium onions, cut into quarters

3 garlic cloves

1 tsp fresh ginger, peeled and grated

2 tbsp (30 ml) vegetable oil or ghee

½ tsp ground cumin

½ tsp ground coriander

1 tsp turmeric

1 tsp garam masala

½ tsp ground cayenne pepper (optional)

Sea salt, to taste

1⅓ cups (320 ml) vegetable stock, warmed, divided

3 canned whole plum tomatoes

2 cans (15.5-oz [440-g]) chickpeas, rinsed and drained

5 cups (150 g) spinach leaves

1 tbsp (15 ml) fresh lemon juice

TO SERVE

1⅔ cups (310 g) steamed jasmine or basmati rice

2 tbsp (2 g) fresh coriander leaves, minced, divided

1 lemon, cut into wedges

We love Indian-style meals, and over the years, this ten-minute chickpea and spinach curry recipe has quickly become a family favorite. It's an easier and quicker version of traditional Indian chana masala and features the most basic cupboard ingredients. It's one of those quick, nutritious meals you can whip up in no time, without planning ahead. It comes together all in one pot, is conveniently gluten-free and overall incredibly simple to prepare.

Place the onions, garlic and ginger in a food processor, and pulse all the ingredients for about 30 seconds, or until you have a creamy but slightly chunky mixture.

Heat a large pan with the oil over medium heat, then add the onion, garlic and ginger mixture and stir-fry it for 2 minutes, until softened.

Stir in the spices and a generous pinch of salt, and cook for an additional 2 minutes, adding a splash of vegetable stock to prevent them from burning.

Add in the tomatoes and continue to cook for another 2 minutes, breaking them up into chunks using a wooden spoon or spatula.

Add in the chickpeas, spinach and the remaining stock, and cook for an additional 2 to 3 minutes until the sauce is slightly thickened.

Turn off the heat, drizzle the curry with the lemon juice and divide it into four bowls.

Divide the rice between bowls, sprinkle ½ tablespoon (0.5 g) of fresh coriander leaves on top of each bowl, and serve the curry with a lemon wedge on the side.

> Cooking Tips: *To give your curry a more authentic touch, add a teaspoon of dried mango powder (amchoor powder). If you can't find garam masala spice mix, substitute it with mild curry powder or a jarred mild curry paste.*

Creamy White Chili Sin Carne

3 tbsp (45 ml) extra-virgin olive oil

1 medium yellow onion, finely chopped

2 garlic cloves, minced

½ jalapeño pepper, minced

3 (15.5-oz [440-g]) cans great northern beans, rinsed and drained

¼ tsp cayenne pepper (or to taste)

1 tsp ground cumin

1 tsp dried oregano

1 tbsp (10 g) all-purpose flour or tapioca flour

1 cup (140 g) frozen corn kernels

1 (4-oz [120-g]) can green chiles

2 cups (480 ml) vegetable stock, warmed

½ cup (120 ml) nondairy milk such as oat or almond milk

¼ tsp sea salt

Freshly cracked black pepper, to taste

TOPPINGS

1 tbsp (1 g) cilantro leaves, finely chopped

1 green onion, finely sliced

1 avocado, diced

1 lime, cut into 4 wedges

4 tbsp (60 ml) vegan sour cream

This cozy, creamy and filling white chili is loaded with nutritious beans, plenty of flavor and just the right amount of kick, so you won't miss the meat at all! This fantastic weeknight meal is ready on the dinner table in just about 30 minutes, making it a great option on a busy day.

Heat a medium stock pot or Dutch oven with the olive oil over low heat. Add in the onion, garlic and jalapeño. Stir often for about 5 minutes, until the veggies have softened.

Add in the beans, followed by the spices, oregano, flour, corn and chiles. Stir all the ingredients for 1 minute, then gently smash one-third of the mixture with a potato masher to help you reach a creamy texture. (Alternatively, you can blend it until you reach a creamy but still chunky texture.)

Pour the stock into the pot, then bring it to a boil and simmer for 15 minutes. Pour the milk into the soup, and continue to simmer all the ingredients for an additional 5 minutes, until the soup is slightly thickened, then season with ¼ teaspoon of sea salt, and add freshly cracked black pepper to taste.

Divide the vegan chili between four bowls, top each one with some of the cilantro, green onion, avocado, lime and sour cream and serve.

Cooking Tip: *For even more creaminess, add in a finely cubed starchy potato and let it cook together with the other ingredients.*

Mung Bean and Coconut Curry

½ cup (100 g) mung beans

5 cups (1 L) fresh water, divided

1 tsp plus a pinch of sea salt, divided

2 medium onions, cut into quarters

3 garlic cloves

1 tsp fresh ginger, peeled and grated

2 tbsp (30 ml) vegetable oil or ghee

½ tsp ground cumin

½ tsp ground coriander

1 tsp turmeric

1 tsp garam masala

1 tsp ground cayenne pepper

1 curry leaf or bay leaf

2 whole plum tomatoes, canned

1 large sweet potato, peeled and cubed

5 cups (150 g) spinach leaves

½ (7-oz [200-ml]) can coconut milk

1 tbsp (15 ml) fresh lime juice

TO SERVE

1⅔ cups (310 g) steamed jasmine or basmati rice

2 tbsp (2 g) fresh cilantro leaves, finely chopped

1 lime, cut into wedges

Curries are a firm family favorite.

They're easy, fairly quick to prepare and are packed with nutrient-rich ingredients that don't sacrifice on flavor. This mung bean and coconut curry is loaded with Indian-inspired flavors and is sure to bring a great satisfying meal to the family table (and leftovers make an excellent lunchbox option too)!

Rinse the mung beans and place them in a large bowl. Cover them with 2 cups (480 ml) of fresh water, sprinkle with 1 teaspoon of sea salt and let them soak for 4 to 5 hours. Drain them and rinse under cool running water, then set them aside.

Place the onions, garlic and ginger in a food processor, and pulse all the ingredients for about 30 seconds, or until you have a creamy but slightly chunky mixture.

Heat a large pan with the oil over medium heat, then add in the onion, garlic and ginger mixture and stir-fry it for 2 minutes, until softened.

Stir in the spices, curry leaf and a generous pinch of sea salt, and cook all the vegetables for an additional 2 minutes, adding a splash of water to prevent them from burning.

Add in the tomatoes and continue to cook for a further 2 minutes, breaking them up into chunks using a wooden spoon or spatula.

Add the soaked mung beans, sweet potato and 3 cups (720 ml) of water into the pan. Turn the heat to high, bring the mixture to a boil, then reduce the heat and simmer for 30 minutes, or until the beans are cooked through and the sweet potato is softened.

Fold the spinach into the pan. Add in the coconut milk, increase the heat to medium-high and cook all the ingredients for an additional 5 minutes.

Turn off the heat, drizzle the curry with the lime juice and divide it into four bowls.

Divide the steamed rice between the bowls, sprinkle cilantro on top of each and serve with a lime wedge on the side.

> **Cooking Tip:** *If you can't find garam masala spice mix, substitute it with mild curry powder or a jarred mild curry paste.*

Traditional Italian Chickpea Pasta Soup

3 tbsp (45 ml) extra-virgin olive oil, divided

1 medium yellow onion, finely chopped

1 carrot, peeled and finely chopped

1 large potato, peeled and finely cubed

1 garlic clove, grated

2 (15.5-oz [440-g]) cans chickpeas, rinsed and drained

1 tbsp (2 g) rosemary leaves, finely chopped

1 tsp thyme leaves, finely chopped

Sea salt and freshly cracked black pepper, to taste

4 cups (960 ml) vegetable stock

9 oz (250 g) short pasta (such as ditali or mezzi rigatoni)

This traditional Italian soup is packed with classic flavors and comes together with simple, inexpensive pantry ingredients, such as nourishing chickpeas, pasta and basic veggies. For a hearty kick, you can substitute the pasta with another wholesome grain such as farro, rice or buckwheat noodles.

Heat 2 tablespoons (30 ml) of olive oil in a large pot over medium heat. Add the onion, carrot and potato, followed by the garlic, chickpeas, rosemary and thyme. Sauté all the vegetables for 5 minutes, or until they begin to soften, adding a splash of water if they begin to brown too much. Season with a generous pinch of sea salt and freshly cracked black pepper to taste.

Pour in the stock, cover the pot with a lid and bring to a boil, then reduce the heat and simmer for 5 to 7 minutes. Add the pasta into the pot, and let it cook for about 10 minutes or until tender to the bite, then adjust the seasoning to taste.

Remove the pot from the heat, and divide the soup between five bowls. Drizzle the remaining 1 tablespoon (15 ml) of olive oil over the top, season with extra freshly cracked black pepper and serve.

Protein-Packed Pasta for Every Day

Because I grew up in Italy, pasta is dear to my heart. On days when I'm not really sure what to cook, I always turn to some type of pasta. It's simple, I'm always in the mood for it and the whole family loves it. Plus, there are endless ways to turn it into a wholesome, satisfying meal.

This awesome chapter features the most flavor-popping, drool-worthy vegan pasta recipes to add to your dinner table. They are all naturally loaded with protein-rich legumes, and you'll even find some helpful hidden-bean recipes for the "I-don't-eat-beans" pasta lovers around the table. This chapter includes my famous Creamy Cannellini Fettuccine Alfredo (page 91), with a creamy, dreamy alfredo sauce made with cannellini beans. I also share crowd-pleasing pasta dishes such as the Sunday Skillet Chickpea Lasagna with Butternut Squash Sauce (page 80). Throw-together options like Quick Tuscan Pasta e Fagioli (page 83) and Penne all'Arrabbiata with White Beans (page 84) are made with the most simple pantry-friendly ingredients. You're going to want to make all of them!

Spaghetti and Bean No-Meatballs

2 tbsp (30 ml) extra-virgin olive oil, divided

½ medium onion, minced

1 garlic clove, grated

2 tbsp (30 g) walnuts, chopped

1 (15.5-oz [440-g]) can black beans, rinsed and drained

1 tbsp (15 g) tomato paste

1 tsp low-sodium soy sauce

2 tbsp (5 g) basil leaves, finely chopped

½ tsp dried oregano

Zest of ½ lemon

1 tbsp (5 g) nutritional yeast

½ cup (45 g) quick oats

Sea salt and freshly cracked black pepper, to taste

13 oz (370 g) spaghetti or other pasta shapes

TOMATO SAUCE

2 tbsp (30 ml) extra-virgin olive oil

2 (14-oz [400-g]) cans plum tomatoes

1 garlic clove

4 basil leaves, divided

A pinch of brown sugar (or 1 bay leaf)

Fine sea salt and freshly cracked black pepper, to taste

This is a comfort food classic easily turned vegan! I've paired my homemade Italian tomato sauce with delicious, cheap and protein-packed black bean meatballs to deliver a great, satisfying meal everyone goes crazy for!

Preheat the oven to 360°F (180°C) and line a baking tray with parchment paper.

Heat 1 tablespoon (15 ml) of olive oil in a large pan or wok over medium heat, then add the onion and cook for about 3 to 4 minutes, or until translucent. Add the garlic, walnuts and beans, and stir-fry them for an additional 2 minutes, then turn the heat off. Transfer the bean mixture in a food processor. Add in the tomato paste, soy sauce, basil, oregano, lemon zest, nutritional yeast and oats. Pulse until reaching a thick mixture, stopping to scrape the sides of the food processor if necessary. Season with ¼ teaspoon (or to taste) of sea salt, and add a generous pinch of freshly cracked black pepper.

Use your hands or an ice cream scoop to form small balls. If the mixture is too wet, add an extra tablespoon (6 g) of oats. Arrange the balls over the prepared baking tray, and brush them with the remaining 1 tablespoon (15 ml) of olive oil. Bake them for 15 minutes, turning them halfway through the baking time. Once ready, remove them from the oven and set them aside until needed.

In the meantime, prepare the spaghetti and the tomato sauce. Fill a large stockpot two-thirds full with lightly salted water and bring to a boil. Heat a separate large saucepan with 2 tablespoons (30 ml) of olive oil. Fold in the tomatoes and their juice, followed by the garlic and stir-fry them for 5 minutes. Add in 2 basil leaves and a pinch of sugar, cover with a lid and cook for 15 minutes.

Discard the garlic and season the sauce with ¼ teaspoon (or to taste) of fine sea salt and a pinch of freshly cracked black pepper, then stir in the prepared meatballs, add the remaining 2 basil leaves, and turn off the heat.

Add the pasta into the pot of boiling water and cook until al dente, according to package directions, about 8 minutes. Drain the pasta and add it into the pan with the tomato and meatball sauce. Stir all the ingredients together and serve.

Cooking Tip: *Make a double batch of no-meatballs and store them in the freezer for a quick dinner option for those days you don't feel like spending too much time in the kitchen.*

Cauliflower Mac & Cheese with a Bean Kick

1 head cauliflower, chopped into small florets

13 oz (370 g) elbow pasta

2 garlic cloves, finely minced

1 tsp red chili flakes

1 tsp smoked paprika

1 (15.5-oz [440-g]) can cannellini beans, rinsed and drained

1 tbsp (15 ml) Dijon mustard

1 tbsp (15 ml) extra-virgin olive oil

1 tbsp (5 g) nutritional yeast (optional)

Sea salt and freshly cracked black pepper, to taste

TOPPING

½ cup (30 g) panko breadcrumbs

1 tbsp (15 ml) extra-virgin olive oil

1 tsp smoked paprika

1 tbsp (1 g) fresh chives, finely chopped

> **Cooking Tip:** *Umami-rich nutritional yeast is an optional ingredient for the sauce, but it gives a nice cheesy flavor and an extra nutritional boost—so if you have it on hand, don't skip it!*

What's more comforting than a big bowl of freshly made mac & cheese on a cold winter night? I'm going to show you how you can easily transform a cheap can of cannellini beans and a head of cauliflower into a creamy, magically dairy-free sauce and turn this classic dish into a protein-rich and so-good-for-you meal.

Bring a large pot of lightly salted water to a boil and, as soon as the water boils, fold in the cauliflower and cook until soft and tender, about 10 minutes. With the help of a slotted spoon, transfer the florets into a blender.

Preheat the oven to 400°F (200°C), and arrange the baking rack onto the middle shelf.

Bring the water in the pot back to a boil, then fold in the pasta and cook until al dente, about 7 minutes. Remove ½ cup (120 ml) of water from the pot and set it aside.

While the pasta cooks, add the garlic, chili flakes, paprika, beans, mustard, olive oil and nutritional yeast (if using) into the blender with the cauliflower, and pulse until it reaches a chunky consistency.

Set the food processor on slow speed, and gently pour in the reserved pasta water, a little at a time, until the sauce reaches a creamy and silky texture, then season with a generous pinch of sea salt and freshly cracked black pepper to taste.

Remove the pot from the heat and drain the pasta. Return the pasta to the pot, stir in the sauce and toss gently to combine all the ingredients.

In a small bowl, prepare the topping. Combine the breadcrumbs with the olive oil and paprika. Transfer the pasta into a large baking dish and top with the panko mixture, then place in the oven and bake until golden and crispy on top, about 10 minutes.

Remove the baking dish from the oven, allow the pasta to cool slightly, then top with freshly chopped chives and serve.

Sunday Skillet Chickpea Lasagna with Butternut Squash Sauce

1 (15.5-oz [440-g]) can chickpeas, rinsed and drained

1½ tsp (3 g) rosemary leaves, minced

1 garlic clove, grated

A pinch of za'atar spice mix

3½ tbsp (55 ml) extra-virgin oil, divided

Sea salt and freshly cracked black pepper, to taste

10–12 dry lasagna sheets

4–5 sage leaves

BUTTERNUT SQUASH SAUCE

15 oz (420 g) butternut squash puree

½ cup (120 ml) rice, oat or almond milk

¼ tsp ground nutmeg

½ tbsp (1 g) sage leaves, minced

Sea salt and freshly cracked black pepper, to taste

Growing up in Italy, I've eaten more lasagna than I could possibly remember! After trying many vegan lasagna recipes, I can definitely call this one a winner. It's easier to make than most lasagna recipes out there, and it surely has it all. This lasagna is creamy thanks to the butternut squash sauce, crunchy and nutrient-rich thanks to the roasted chickpeas and absolutely comforting thanks to all these amazing fall flavors together.

Preheat the oven to 430°F (220°C), and arrange the baking rack onto the middle shelf.

Place the chickpeas on paper towels and pat them dry, removing any loose skin. Line a baking tray with parchment paper, and add the chickpeas, followed by the rosemary, garlic, za'atar, 1½ tablespoons (25 ml) of olive oil and ¼ teaspoon (or to taste) of sea salt.

Toss all the ingredients well with a spoon to evenly coat the chickpeas, then spread them in a single layer.

Transfer the tray to the oven, and roast them for 20 minutes, or until slightly crispy. Stir them halfway through the baking time, then remove from the oven and set them aside until needed.

For the butternut squash sauce, pour the puree into a large bowl and slowly whisk in the milk until reaching a creamy, velvety consistency. Season with nutmeg, sage and a generous pinch of sea salt and freshly cracked black pepper, then set it aside until needed.

RICOTTA SAUCE

1 cup (250 g) vegan ricotta-style cheese

⅔ cup (160 ml) rice, oat or almond milk

⅔ cup (65 g) vegan Parmesan-style cheese, grated

A pinch of nutmeg

Sea salt and freshly cracked black pepper, to taste

For the ricotta mixture, place the ricotta-style cheese in a large bowl, and slowly whisk in the milk until reaching a creamy consistency. Incorporate the Parmesan-style cheese, season with a generous pinch of nutmeg, sea salt and freshly cracked black pepper, and set it aside until needed.

In the meantime, bring a large pot of lightly salted water to a boil, place 2 lasagna sheets at a time into the pot and blanch them for 2 minutes, then line them on a clean kitchen cloth and repeat the process with the remaining lasagna sheets.

Drizzle 1 tablespoon (15 ml) of olive oil into a 10-inch (25-cm) cast-iron skillet, then layer 3 to 4 lasagna sheets over the bottom, overlapping them slightly.

Spread one-third of the butternut squash sauce over the pasta, followed by half of the baked chickpeas, and top with one-third of the ricotta mixture.

Repeat the process with one more layer of lasagna sheets, followed by the one-third of butternut squash sauce, then the other half of the chickpeas and then one-third of ricotta mixture.

Layer the remaining lasagna sheets over the top, and spread the remaining ricotta mixture and butternut squash sauce over the top. Drizzle it with the remaining 1 tablespoon (15 ml) of olive oil. Lower the oven temperature to 360°F (180°C), then bake the lasagna for 15 to 20 minutes, until the edges are nicely golden and the sauce is gently bubbling.

Remove the lasagna from the oven, sprinkle fresh sage leaves and freshly cracked black pepper over the top and serve.

*See photo on page 74.

Cooking Tip: *To bring even more flavor to the sauce, try making your homemade roasted butternut squash puree. Cube half a butternut squash and arrange it with half a chopped onion on a baking tray covered with parchment paper, drizzle with 1 tablespoon (15 ml) of extra-virgin olive oil and season with a generous pinch of sea salt and freshly cracked black pepper. Toss to coat the cubes, and spread them on a single layer on the baking tray. Roast them in the oven for 30 to 35 minutes, then transfer into a blender. Blend until smooth and store in the refrigerator until needed.*

Quick Tuscan Pasta e Fagioli

3 tbsp (45 ml) extra-virgin olive oil, divided

1 shallot, minced

2 (15-oz [440-g]) cans borlotti beans, rinsed and drained

2 sage leaves, finely chopped

1 tbsp (2 g) rosemary leaves, finely chopped

4 cups (960 ml) hot vegetable stock, divided

Fine sea salt and freshly cracked black pepper, to taste

12 oz (350 g) short pasta such as ditali or mezzi rigatoni

2 tbsp (11 g) vegan Parmesan-style cheese, grated (optional)

Borlotti are super popular beans in Italy and make the base for a vast array of soups and pasta recipes. Traditional recipes call for dried borlotti, but if you opt for the jarred or canned version, you'll get this comforting and nourishing pasta soup ready in barely 15 minutes. Trust me, it will taste incredible and look like you have spent hours on it!

Heat 2 tablespoons (30 ml) of olive oil in large pan over medium-low heat. Add the shallot and cook until it begins to turn golden, adding a bit of warm water if necessary.

Add in the beans, sage and rosemary, pour in half the stock and simmer for 5 minutes. Stir occasionally, then season with ½ teaspoon (or to taste) of fine sea salt and a pinch of freshly cracked black pepper.

Transfer half of the bean soup mixture into a blender, blend it until smooth and return it into the pot. Pour the remaining stock into the pot, add in the pasta and cook, stirring occasionally, until the pasta is cooked through, for about 7 minutes.

Divide the pasta between four bowls, top them with grated vegan Parmesan-style cheese and freshly cracked black pepper, drizzle with the remaining olive oil and serve.

Cooking Tip: *Borlotti beans are also called cranberry beans in the United States. If you can't find them, feel free to substitute them with pinto beans.*

Penne all'Arrabbiata with White Beans

3 tbsp (45 ml) extra-virgin olive oil, divided

2 garlic cloves, whole

2 medium hot chilies, seeded and finely sliced

2 (14-oz [400-g]) cans plum tomatoes

4 basil leaves, divided

A pinch of brown sugar (or 1 bay leaf)

1 (15.5-oz [440-g]) can white beans, rinsed and drained

Fine sea salt and freshly cracked black pepper, to taste

13 oz (370 g) penne pasta

An Italian classic that never goes out of fashion. Fiercely spicy, with added nutritional value thanks to the inclusion of buttery white beans, this is a super easy and satisfying meal, perfect for busy weekdays or to please a large and hungry crowd.

Fill two-thirds of a large stockpot with lightly salted water and bring to a boil.

Heat a large saucepan with 2 tablespoons (30 ml) of olive oil, garlic and chilies over medium-low heat. Fold in the tomatoes and their juice, and sauté them for 5 minutes.

Add in 2 basil leaves and a pinch of sugar, cover with a lid and cook for 10 to 15 minutes. Halfway through the cooking time, add in the beans and continue to cook the sauce over low heat.

Discard the garlic and season the sauce with ¼ teaspoon (or to taste) of fine sea salt and a pinch of freshly cracked black pepper.

Add the pasta into the pot of boiling water and cook until al dente, according to package directions, for about 8 minutes. Drain the pasta and add it into the pan with the tomato-based sauce, followed by the remaining basil leaves. Stir all the ingredients together, swirl the remaining 1 tablespoon (15 ml) of olive oil over the top and serve.

> **Cooking Tip:** *Feel free to substitute white beans with borlotti beans if you like; they work amazingly well too!*

Best Black Bean Spaghetti Bolognese

3 tbsp (45 ml) extra-virgin olive oil

1 medium yellow onion, finely chopped

1 carrot, finely cubed

1 celery stalk, finely cubed

5 oz (140 g) fresh shiitake mushrooms, finely chopped

1 (15.5-oz [440-g]) can black beans, rinsed and drained

½ cup (95 g) dried red lentils, rinsed and drained

¾ cup (180 ml) vegan dry white wine

3 tbsp (45 g) double concentrate tomato paste

1 bay leaf

1 cup (240 ml) vegetable stock, warmed

1 tbsp (15 g) plus ¼ tsp sea salt, divided

Freshly cracked black pepper, to taste

12 oz (350 g) spaghetti

My go-to plant-based spaghetti Bolognese is built from the authentic Italian recipe, but it swaps the meat with convenient and protein-rich black beans for a hearty, satisfying meal. Whether you need to impress a date or your family, this vegan take on classic Bolognese is sure to wow your table companions.

Heat a medium-large stock pot or Dutch oven with the olive oil over low heat. Add in the onion, carrot, celery and mushrooms and cook for about 5 minutes, stirring often, until the veggies have softened.

Add in the beans and lentils, then pour in the wine. Stir all the ingredients together for 2 minutes.

Stir in the tomato paste followed by the bay leaf, then pour the stock into the pot, bring to a gentle boil and simmer for 15 to 20 minutes over low heat.

In the meantime, fill two-thirds of a large stockpot with water and bring to a boil. As soon as the water boils, add roughly 1 tablespoon (15 g) of fine sea salt, fold in the spaghetti and cook until al dente, about 7 to 8 minutes.

Discard the bay leaf from the Bolognese sauce and season with ¼ teaspoon (or to taste) of sea salt and freshly cracked black pepper to taste. Drain the pasta and transfer it into the pot with the sauce. Stir to combine all the ingredients, then divide the pasta between the plates and serve.

Cooking Tip: *Feeling cheesy? Top this classic pasta with a few dollops of vegan ricotta or dust with freshly-grated Parmesan-style vegan cheese just before serving.*

Creamy Edamame Pesto Pasta

10 oz (280 g) edamame beans

½ cup (67 g) garden peas, frozen

13 oz (370 g) spaghetti or other pasta shapes

1 handful fresh basil leaves

½ cup (54 g) toasted slivered almonds

1 garlic clove, grated

Zest and juice of 1 lemon

¼ cup (60 ml) extra-virgin olive oil

Sea salt and freshly cracked black pepper, to taste

TO SERVE

1 tbsp (7 g) toasted slivered almonds

Zest of ½ lemon

1 handful of basil leaves

Freshly cracked black pepper

Cooking Tip: *Feeling cheesy? Top this vibrant pasta with a few dollops of fresh vegan ricotta or vegan Parmesan-style cheese just before serving.*

A new, delicious version of the classic Italian basil pesto, this vibrant sauce features nutrient-packed edamame beans. Loaded with healthy goodness and ready in less than twenty minutes, this awesomely vegan pesto sauce goes beautifully tossed with pasta, but it can deliver so much more. Serve it with crudités, homemade tortilla chips, add a spoonful or two to any of the salads or burger recipes featured in this book or simply enjoy it with warm and crunchy toasted bread.

Bring a large pot of lightly salted water to a boil and, as soon as the water boils, fold in the edamame and peas and cook for 4 minutes, until slightly tender and bright green.

With the help of a slotted spoon, transfer the vegetables from the water into a bowl with cold water and ice. Let them sit for 2 minutes, then drain and set aside.

Bring the pot of water used for cooking the vegetables back to a boil, fold in the pasta and cook until al dente, about 7 to 8 minutes for spaghetti. Remove ¼ cup (60 ml) of water from the pot and set aside before straining.

While the pasta is cooking, place the edamame, peas, basil, almonds, garlic and lemon zest and juice into a food processor and pulse until reaching a chunky consistency.

Set the food processor on slow speed and gently pour in the olive oil, then continue to mix on medium-high speed for about 2 minutes, or until the edamame pesto reaches a creamy and dense texture.

Slowly pour the reserved cooking water into the edamame pesto, continuing to mix until reaching the desired consistency. Season with sea salt and freshly cracked black pepper to taste.

Remove the pot from the heat and drain the pasta. Return the pasta to the pot, stir in the edamame pesto and toss gently to combine all the ingredients.

Serve immediately with toasted almonds, lemon zest, basil and freshly cracked black pepper on top.

Creamy Cannellini Fettuccine Alfredo

2 tbsp (30 ml) extra-virgin olive oil

½ yellow onion, minced

2 garlic cloves, finely sliced

1 tsp red chili flakes

1 (15.5-oz [440-g]) can cannellini or navy beans, rinsed and drained

Juice of 1 lemon

1 tbsp (5 g) nutritional yeast

1 cup (240 ml) vegetable stock, hot

Sea salt and freshly cracked black pepper, to taste

13 oz (370 g) fettuccine or other pasta shapes

TO SERVE

Zest of ½ lemon

1 handful of parsley leaves, finely chopped

Freshly cracked black pepper

Who would have ever guessed that you can turn a can of white beans into a delicious and creamy alfredo sauce? This vegan take on the classic American favorite is healthy, speedy, nutritious and totally guilt-free!

Heat the olive oil in a large skillet over medium-low heat. Add the onion and stir-fry for 2 minutes or until just soft. Then add in the garlic, chili flakes and beans and continue to cook for an additional 5 minutes, until the vegetables have softened, adding a splash of water if necessary.

Transfer the sautéed bean mixture into a food processor. Add in the lemon juice and nutritional yeast, and pulse until it reaches a chunky consistency.

Set the food processor on slow speed and gently pour in the stock, a little at a time, and continue to blend until the sauce reaches a creamy texture. Season with a generous pinch of sea salt and freshly cracked black pepper to taste.

Bring a large pot of lightly salted water to a boil, and as soon as the water boils, fold in the pasta and cook until al dente, about 7 to 8 minutes for fettuccine. Remove ¼ cup (60 ml) of water from the pot and set aside.

Remove the pot from the heat and drain the pasta. Return the pasta to the pot, stir in the vegan alfredo sauce and toss gently to combine all the ingredients, adding a little of the reserved pasta water until reaching a velvety sauce consistency.

Top the fettuccine with lemon zest, chopped parsley and freshly cracked black pepper and serve.

> **Cooking Tip:** *Umami-rich nutritional yeast is a key ingredient in the sauce, as it provides a cheesy flavor, so it's worth picking up even if it's not one of your pantry staples.*

Vibrant and Wholesome Pulse Salads and Sides

It's all about the sides—and I'm not talking sad-looking green salads and bland steamed veggies. I'm talking unique vegan side dishes and vibrant salads that bring together seasonal veggies, protein-rich beans and a handful of other flavor-packed ingredients that deliver big and are fuss-free to make.

This chapter will prove that it is incredibly easy to turn inexpensive and nourishing legumes into drool-worthy, creative and nutritious sides and salads.

From classic Weeknight Baked Beans (page 99) to Sneaky Navy Bean Potato Mash (page 103) to nutrient-packed Quinoa and Beans Power Salad (page 100), these dishes are so delicious! Everyone—meat eaters included—will want to try them. They're perfect for accompanying weeknight meals and special occasions alike. (Hello, Thanksgiving, Christmas and summer BBQs!) Plus, they pair with just about any main course featured in the previous chapters!

Super Quick Greek-Style Chickpea Salad

1 tbsp (15 ml) fresh lemon juice

2 tbsp (30 ml) extra-virgin olive oil

1 garlic clove, grated

1 (15.5-oz [440-g]) can chickpeas, rinsed and drained

5 oz (150 g) mixed cherry tomatoes, halved

1 medium cucumber, diced

½ red onion, finely sliced

⅔ cup (100 g) vegan feta-style cheese, crumbled (optional)

1 tbsp (1 g) fresh basil leaves, chopped

1 tsp freshly dried oregano leaves

Sea salt and freshly cracked black pepper, to taste

I could make this five-minute salad over and over again and never get tired of it! Greek-style salad is a must in summertime, and I love powering it up with some chickpeas. They are super cheap, easy to find and store and keep you full for longer. The beauty of this salad is its versatility. You can whip it together in a flash and bring it to work, potlucks, picnics or dinner parties. This salad works perfectly as a side dish, but if you want to make it a meal, just throw in your favorite cooked grain—couscous, quinoa, pasta or wild rice. The sky is the limit!

In a small jar, add the lemon juice, olive oil and garlic. Close the lid and shake it well until all ingredients are combined.

In a large bowl, add in the chickpeas, tomatoes, cucumber, onion, cheese, basil and oregano. Pour the prepared dressing all over the salad, then toss everything together. Season with ¼ teaspoon (or to taste) of sea salt and freshly cracked black pepper and serve.

> Cooking Tip: *Feel free to play with different beans for this salad! White beans, kidney beans and black-eyed peas are some delicious alternatives that would work just as well in this refreshing summer dish.*

Mexican-Style Three-Bean Salad

1 (15.5-oz [440-g]) can pinto beans, rinsed and drained

1 (15.5-oz [440-g]) can black beans, rinsed and drained

1 (15.5-oz [440-g]) can cannellini beans, rinsed and drained

1 cup (150 g) frozen corn, thawed

1 medium red onion, minced

1 garlic clove, minced

1 avocado, diced

½ large yellow bell pepper, finely chopped

½ large red bell pepper, finely chopped

1 jalapeño pepper, seeded and finely chopped

1 tbsp (1 g) fresh cilantro leaves, chopped

1 tbsp (15 ml) fresh lime juice

2 tbsp (30 ml) extra-virgin olive oil

1 tsp ground cumin

Sea salt and freshly cracked black pepper, to taste

This Mexican-style three bean salad is full of healthy veggies and cheap and nutritious canned beans that you probably already have in your pantry. Serve it as a wholesome side dish or make it the star of your dinner by using it as a filling for baked potatoes, wraps, tacos or sandwich bread for a tasty meat-free meal.

In a large bowl, mix together the beans, corn, onion, garlic, avocado, bell peppers, jalapeño and cilantro.

In a small jar, whisk together the lime juice, olive oil, cumin and ½ teaspoon (or to taste) of sea salt and a pinch of freshly cracked black pepper.

Drizzle the prepared dressing all over the salad, toss and serve.

Cooking Tip: *If you're making this salad in advance, omit the avocado during assembly and add it just before serving to prevent it from browning.*

Weeknight Baked Beans

1 tbsp (15 ml) extra-virgin olive oil

½ onion, finely minced

2 garlic cloves, minced

1 tbsp (15 g) tomato paste

1 tbsp (15 ml) maple syrup

A pinch of dried thyme

½ tsp smoked paprika

1 tbsp (15 ml) low sodium soy sauce or tamari

1 tsp vegan Worcestershire sauce (optional)

½ cup (110 g) pureed tomatoes or tomato passata

1 (15.5-oz [440-g]) can cannellini beans, rinsed and drained

A pinch of freshly cracked black pepper

Ditch the store-bought canned version and make your own healthier and cheaper baked beans in a flash. Try this delicious and super quick recipe, and serve your homemade baked beans on toast, with baked potatoes or with a large salad.

Heat the olive oil in a saucepan over medium-low heat. Then add the onion and garlic and cook, stirring often, until they're soft, about 5 minutes. Add in the tomato paste followed by the maple syrup, thyme, paprika, soy sauce, Worcestershire sauce (if using) and pureed tomatoes. Stir well and cook all the ingredients for an additional 2 minutes.

Add the beans into the saucepan and simmer all the ingredients for 6 to 8 minutes over low heat, until the sauce has thickened slightly. Adjust the seasoning by adding a pinch of freshly cracked black pepper, then remove the pan from the heat and serve your baked beans nice and hot.

Cooking Tip: *Baked beans freeze great! Divide any leftovers into portions and store them in the freezer for a handy meal whenever you don't feel like cooking.*

Quinoa and Beans Power Salad

1 cup (185 g) cooked quinoa

1 large cucumber, diced

1 cup (150 g) mixed cherry tomatoes, halved

5 oz (150 g) baby spinach leaves, chopped

1 medium red onion, minced

1 tbsp (1 g) fresh basil leaves, chopped

1 tbsp (1 g) fresh mint leaves, chopped

1 (15.5-oz [440-g]) can chickpeas, rinsed and drained

½ (7-oz [200 g]) can black beans, rinsed and drained

½ (7 oz [200 g]) can cannellini beans, rinsed and drained

DRESSING

2 tbsp (30 ml) extra-virgin olive oil

1 tbsp (15 ml) fresh lemon juice

1 tsp Dijon mustard

1 tbsp (15 ml) apple cider vinegar

1 tsp maple syrup

1 garlic clove, grated

Sea salt and freshly cracked black pepper, to taste

This superfood salad is a nutritional powerhouse featuring healthy quinoa, three different kinds of beans and loads of refreshing veggies. This is one of my favorite lunchbox or potluck options when I'm in a hurry!

In a large bowl, add in the quinoa, cucumber, tomatoes, spinach, onion, basil, mint and beans, and mix to combine.

In a small jar, whisk together the olive oil, lemon juice, mustard, vinegar, maple syrup, garlic, ½ teaspoon (or to taste) of sea salt and a generous pinch of freshly cracked black pepper. Close the jar with a lid and shake it to combine all the ingredients.

Pour the prepared dressing all over the quinoa salad, mix all the ingredients to combine and serve.

Cooking Tip: *This awesome salad works well with tons of different veggies! Try adding grilled corn, avocado, red cabbage, carrots or broccoli for even more flavor.*

Sneaky Navy Bean Potato Mash

4–6 (17 oz [500 g]) medium russet or Yukon Gold potatoes

1 tsp fine sea salt, plus more to taste

1 (15.5-oz [440-g]) can navy beans, rinsed and drained

3 tbsp (45 ml) extra-virgin olive oil

½ cup (120 ml) vegetable stock, hot

1 tsp fresh thyme leaves

1 tsp lemon zest

A pinch of grated nutmeg

Freshly cracked black pepper, to taste

Loved by grown-ups and kids alike, mashed potatoes make a super versatile side dish for both weeknight meals and festive dinners. When I make mine, I like to sneak in some wholesome navy beans, and I promise you they go completely undetected, while adding an extra kick of high-quality plant protein.

Place the potatoes in a large pot, cover with cold water and add the fine sea salt. Bring to a boil, then simmer for about 20 minutes, or until the potatoes are tender and cooked through. Once the potatoes are ready, drain them in a colander and peel them while still hot.

Transfer the potatoes to a large bowl, add the beans and olive oil and mash the ingredients with a potato masher.

Slowly pour the stock in and continue to mash the potatoes and beans until they reach the desired texture.

Season with fresh thyme, lemon zest, nutmeg, more sea salt and freshly cracked black pepper to taste and serve.

Cooking Tip: *For a creamier texture, you can mash the potatoes using a potato ricer. This helpful tool will also save you time, as you don't need to peel the potatoes beforehand.*

Winter Cannellini Farro Salad

8 oz (230 g) whole-grain farro

1 small butternut squash, peeled, seeded and cubed

2 tbsp (30 ml) extra-virgin olive oil, divided

Sea salt and freshly cracked black pepper, to taste

4 oz (120 g) curly kale, ribs removed and chopped

5 oz (150 g) cooked cannellini beans, rinsed and drained

¼ cup (30 g) dried cranberries

¼ cup (30 g) almond flakes, toasted

Juice of 1 lemon

This hearty winter salad features protein-packed cannellini beans and wholesome, chewy farro combined with crunchy kale, sweet almonds, cranberries and butternut squash. This is a perfect feel-good salad that you can eat during the colder months over and over again without getting bored!

Preheat the oven to 390°F (200°C) and line a large baking tray with parchment paper.

Bring a pot of lightly salted water to a boil. Place the farro into a fine mesh sieve, and rinse it well under cold running water. Drain the farro, place into the boiling water and cook for about 20 minutes, or until it's just tender. Drain and set it aside until needed.

Arrange the butternut squash cubes on the prepared baking tray, drizzle with 1 tablespoon (15 ml) of olive oil and season with a generous pinch of sea salt and freshly cracked black pepper. Toss to coat the cubes and spread them on a single layer on the baking tray. Roast them in the oven for 30 to 35 minutes, or until they're tender, cooked through and slightly browned around the edges.

Place the kale in a large bowl, drizzle it with the remaining 1 tablespoon (15 ml) of olive oil and sprinkle with a generous pinch of sea salt, then massage it with your hands by pinching it and squeezing it for a couple of minutes until it softens. When you massage the kale before mixing it in a salad, you are breaking it down so that it is more easily digestible and easier to eat, and also making it less bitter.

Remove the butternut squash from the oven, allow it to cool slightly, then transfer it into the bowl with the kale, followed by the farro, beans, cranberries and almond flakes. Drizzle the lemon juice all over the salad, taste to adjust the seasoning and serve.

> Cooking Tip: *This warm salad works well with other beans, too! My favorite alternatives to cannellini beans are black-eyed peas, chickpeas and butter beans.*

Tutti Bean Bulgur Tabbouleh

SERVINGS:
4

½ cup (70 g) bulgur wheat

1 (15.5-oz [440-g]) can pinto beans, rinsed and drained

1 (15.5-oz [440-g]) can chickpeas, rinsed and drained

1 (15.5-oz [440-g]) can cannellini beans, rinsed and drained

2 Roma tomatoes, seeded and finely cubed

2 green onions, finely sliced

2 cups (60 g) fresh curly parsley leaves, chopped

3 tbsp (20 g) fresh mint leaves, finely chopped

¼ cup (60 ml) fresh lemon juice

¼ cup (60 ml) extra-virgin olive oil

Sea salt and freshly cracked black pepper, to taste

This classic tabbouleh is made even more nutritious thanks to the addition of a healthy and inexpensive medley of canned beans! I make this salad at least once a week during summertime and never get tired of it. It's loaded with vibrant herbs, citrusy flavor and protein-rich beans, making it a fantastic option for a quick summer main course or side dish.

In a small bowl, place the bulgur and cover with 1 inch (2.5 cm) of hot water. Set the bowl aside, and let the bulgur soak until slightly softened but still chewy, about 20 minutes, then drain it well.

In a large bowl, mix the beans, followed by the bulgur, tomatoes, green onions, parsley and mint. Pour the lemon juice and olive oil all over the salad, season with ½ teaspoon (or to taste) of sea salt and add a generous pinch of freshly cracked black pepper.

Stir the salad well to combine all the ingredients and serve it chilled or at room temperature.

Cooking Tip: *If you can't find bulgur, substitute it with couscous. It will be just as delicious!*

Easy Refried Beans

2 tbsp (30 ml) extra-virgin olive oil

½ medium onion, finely chopped

2 cloves of garlic, finely minced

1 tsp chili powder

A pinch of ground cumin (or to taste)

2 (15.5-oz [440-g]) cans pinto beans, rinsed and drained

½ cup (120 ml) vegetable stock, hot

Sea salt and freshly cracked black pepper, to taste

2 tbsp (2 g) fresh cilantro leaves, chopped

There's no need to buy canned refried beans when you can make your own in just about twenty minutes! This easy, healthy and low-cost side dish is sure to spice up any Mexican-style weeknight meal. As an added bonus, it's conveniently gluten-free!

Heat the olive oil in medium saucepan over medium-low heat, add the onion and cook for about 5 minutes, or until tender and translucent. Stir in the garlic, chili powder and cumin and continue to cook for an additional 2 minutes, adding a splash of water if the garlic begins to brown too much.

Add the beans and stock and continue to cook, stirring often, for about 5 minutes, or until the beans are warmed through.

Reduce the heat to minimum and mash the beans using a potato masher or the back of a wooden spoon until reaching the desired consistency. Season with ¼ teaspoon (or to taste) of fine sea salt and a pinch of freshly cracked black pepper. If the bean mixture seems too dry, stir in a splash of warm water until you reach your desired consistency.

Remove the pan from the heat, stir in the cilantro leaves and serve warm.

Cooking Tip: *Feel free to add the juice of half a lime for a vibrant and refreshing note.*

Asian-Style Edamame and Veggie Noodle Salad

9 oz (255 g) soba noodles or spaghetti

2 cups (260 g) edamame beans

¼ purple cabbage, cored and thinly sliced

1 cup (125 g) mung bean sprouts or microgreens

1 carrot, peeled and finely sliced or coarsely grated

½ red bell pepper, cored and seeded, thinly sliced

2 green onions, thinly sliced

½ cucumber, peeled and finely sliced or finely cubed

3 tbsp (6 g) fresh cilantro leaves, finely chopped

¼ cup (40 g) unsalted dry roasted peanuts, chopped

DRESSING

2 tbsp (30 ml) extra-virgin olive oil or vegetable oil

2 tbsp (30 ml) low-sodium soy sauce or tamari

1 tbsp (15 ml) toasted sesame oil

1 garlic clove, grated

1 tsp (5 g) fresh ginger, grated

1 tbsp (15 ml) maple syrup

1 medium hot chili, seeded and finely minced

Juice of 1 small lime

This is a healthy, colorful salad packed with nutritious edamame and mung bean sprouts, veggies and Asian-inspired flavors. Don't be strict on the choice of the vegetables: Broccoli, white cabbage and yellow peppers are just a few other options you can add into the mix.

Fill two-thirds of a large stockpot with water and bring to a boil. As soon as the water boils, add the noodles and let them cook for the time prescribed on your noodle package, about 5 minutes for soba and 7 minutes for spaghetti. Halfway through the cooking time, add in the edamame. Transfer the noodles and edamame into a colander, rinse under cool running water, drain and transfer them into a large bowl.

Add the cabbage, bean sprouts, carrot, bell pepper, green onions, cucumber, cilantro and peanuts into the bowl with the noodles, and mix all the ingredients together.

In a small jar, whisk together the olive oil, soy sauce, sesame oil, garlic, ginger, maple syrup, chili and lime juice. Adjust the seasoning, adding a splash of extra soy sauce or maple syrup according to taste.

Pour the prepared dressing all over the salad, mix all the ingredients together and serve.

Cooking Tip: *You can serve this awesome salad cold or at room temperature and store any leftovers in the refrigerator for up to 2 days.*

Crunchy Chickpea Waldorf Salad

½ cup (120 ml) vegan mayonnaise

1 tsp lemon juice

1 tsp maple syrup

2 large Honeycrisp or Fuji apples, cored and cubed

3 celery stalks, cubed

1 (15.5-oz [440-g]) can chickpeas, rinsed and drained

½ cup (80 g) red grapes, halved

½ cup (60 g) walnuts, chopped

¼ cup (30 g) pecans, chopped

Sea salt and freshly cracked black pepper, to taste

This is my vegan take on the classic Waldorf salad! This satisfying evergreen dish truly has it all. It's crunchy, creamy and refreshing and has a nice protein boost thanks to the nutritious chickpeas. Best of all, you just need to toss all the ingredients together, making it a super quick and healthy lunch option.

In a small bowl, whisk together the mayonnaise, lemon juice and maple syrup until all the ingredients are combined.

In a large bowl, add in the apples, celery, chickpeas, grapes, walnuts and pecans. Pour the prepared dressing all over the salad, then toss everything together, season with ¼ teaspoon (or to taste) of sea salt, and add freshly cracked black pepper to taste and serve.

Cooking Tip: *Feel free to play with different beans! For this salad, I find that chickpeas and black-eyed peas are my favorite options in terms of flavor and texture.*

Bean-Boosted Snacks for Any Time of the Day

Who doesn't love snacking? This chapter embraces all my favorite savory snacks using the humble bean. If you think beans are just for dinner, I'm here to prove to you that there are a ton of fun ways to make beans snack-worthy material.

This is the ultimate collection of quick, easy and nutritious snack ideas that you can throw together any time of the day—from breakfast up until midnight. Most of the snacks featured here will fill you up just enough to get you through your next meal and are perfect to share too!

Moreover, these healthy little treats can easily become brunch, lunch or dinner in a snap . . . for those times you don't feel like doing too much cooking. Take the Broad Bean and Zucchini Meatballs (page 126) for example. They definitely scream happy hour, but they are equally incredible tossed with pasta and can easily turn into a satisfying main course paired with a salad or a couple of side dishes.

I'm sure you'll have plenty of fun giving these tasty snacks a try. Don't be afraid to add in your favorite flavors and change things up according to the season. For example, get creative and turn the Spring-Perfect Socca Pizza (page 117) into a year-round snack. Top it up with anything you like and make an exciting new dish every single time.

Spring-Perfect Socca Pizza

SERVINGS:
4

7 oz (200 ml) warm water

1⅓ cups (120 g) chickpea flour

2 tbsp (30 ml) extra-virgin olive oil, divided

½ tsp ground cumin

Sea salt and freshly cracked black pepper, to taste

TOPPINGS

1 avocado, sliced

1 handful of baby greens, such as arugula and/or microgreens

2 radishes, finely sliced

1 tbsp (15 ml) sriracha sauce

French Socca is a naturally gluten-free, high-protein flatbread made from chickpeas that has become hugely popular in recent years. I like to season the batter with a pinch of ground cumin, but feel free to get adventurous! Stir in a little za'atar, garam masala, rosemary or thyme for different flavors. The same goes for the toppings—use this pizza-like base as your blank canvas, and top it with anything you can dream of.

Place the water in a large bowl and slowly whisk in the flour until fully incorporated, then whisk in 1 tablespoon (15 ml) of olive oil. Season with the ground cumin, ¼ teaspoon of sea salt and freshly cracked black pepper to taste. Whisk gently to combine all the ingredients, until the batter has reached a lump-free, velvety consistency. Cover the bowl and refrigerate for at least 30 minutes or up to 2 hours.

Preheat the oven to 430°F (220°C), and arrange the baking tray onto the middle shelf.

Heat a 10-inch (25-cm) oven-safe cast-iron or metal skillet over medium-low heat, then brush with the remaining 1 tablespoon (15 ml) of olive oil and pour in the batter.

Transfer the skillet to the oven, and bake for about 15 minutes, or until the top is slightly golden brown and the edges have browned nicely. Remove the skillet from the oven, allow to cool slightly, then gently loosen the bottom of the socca with a spatula and transfer it onto a wood board or serving plate.

Top the socca with sliced avocado, baby greens and radishes. Drizzle with sriracha sauce and serve.

> Cooking Tip: *You can store the socca pizza base in the refrigerator up to 3 days, then reheat it in the oven at 360°F (180°C) for about 5 minutes.*

No-Tuna Chickpea Salad Sandwich

1 (15.5-oz [440-g]) can chickpeas, rinsed and drained

1 nori sheet, finely chopped

1 celery stalk, finely cubed

1 small red onion, finely cubed

1 tbsp (8 g) capers, finely chopped

1 tbsp (15 ml) Dijon mustard

4 tbsp (60 ml) vegan mayonnaise

Sea salt and freshly cracked black pepper, to taste

4 butter lettuce leaves

1 large tomato, sliced

1 handful of baby greens or sprouts

8 slices of sandwich bread

This sandwich has "eat me" written all over it! It's a fantastic lunchbox option (but is great for breakfast too!), conveniently packed with plant-based protein and it comes together in just ten minutes.

Place the chickpeas in a large bowl and mash them through with a potato masher or fork. Add in the chopped nori, celery, onion, capers, mustard and mayonnaise, and mix all ingredients until combined.

Taste the salad and adjust the seasoning by adding a generous pinch (or to taste) of sea salt and freshly cracked black pepper.

Arrange the lettuce leaves, tomato slices and baby greens on top of four bread slices. Divide the chickpea salad on top of the veggies and top them with the remaining slices of bread.

Cooking Tip: *I love capers preserved in dry sea salt rather than brined. In both cases, make sure to rinse them properly and pat them dry before chopping them.*

Easy, Nourishing Edamame Falafel

2½ cups (420 g) edamame beans

½ yellow onion, minced

1 garlic clove, grated

3 tbsp (10 g) fresh flat-leaf parsley leaves, finely chopped

3 tbsp (3 g) fresh cilantro leaves, finely chopped

Zest of ½ lemon

1 tbsp (10 g) sesame seeds

¼ tsp ground cumin

A pinch of chili powder

¼ tsp fine sea salt

Freshly cracked black pepper

2 tbsp (12 g) chickpea flour

Vegetable oil, for shallow frying, such as grapeseed, sunflower, avocado, canola or peanut oil

Traditional falafel calls for chickpeas, but my version uses edamame for a higher protein swap. The patties are deliciously crispy on the outside and soft and bright green on the inside. Serve them plain with my Extra Creamy Classic Hummus (page 129) or make a falafel pita sandwich or wrap.

Transfer the edamame to a food processor and pulse until you reach a crumbly texture, about 2 minutes, scraping down the sides of the food processor when necessary.

Add in the onion, garlic, parsley, cilantro, lemon zest, sesame seeds, cumin, chili powder and salt, then blend all the ingredients until smooth, about 3 to 4 minutes. Season the mixture with a generous pinch of freshly cracked black pepper, then taste to adjust the seasoning, adding more sea salt as needed.

Add in the chickpea flour, then pulse again to combine all the ingredients. Transfer the mixture into a bowl, cover with a lid and refrigerate for 30 minutes.

Use your hands or an ice cream scoop to form small balls or patties. If the mixture is too wet, add an extra tablespoon (6 g) of chickpea flour. If it's too dry, add a tablespoon (15 ml) of water.

Heat 3 inches (8 cm) of oil in a small frying pan over medium-low heat, until it reaches 350°F (175°C). Fry the patties in small batches at a time and cook them undisturbed for 2 minutes on each side, or until they are nicely crispy and golden brown.

Remove them with a slotted spoon and transfer them to a plate covered with paper towels to absorb any excess oil. Repeat the process with the remaining falafel, then transfer them onto a large plate and serve.

Cooking Tip: *For a healthier version, you can bake the falafel in an oven preheated to 400°F (200°C). Place them on a baking tray covered with parchment paper and bake them for 20 to 30 minutes, flipping them over halfway through the baking time.*

Black-Eyed Pea Fritters with Garlic Dip

1 (15.5-oz [440-g]) can black-eyed peas, rinsed and drained

1 small potato, peeled and steamed

2 green onions, finely sliced

¼ cup (35 g) frozen corn, thawed

2 tbsp (2 g) fresh parsley leaves, chopped

1 garlic clove, grated

½ small zucchini, finely grated

½ cup (60 g) oat flour

1 tsp smoked paprika

Sea salt and freshly cracked black pepper, to taste

Vegetable oil, for frying

GARLIC DIP

½ cup (120 ml) plain soy yogurt

2 garlic cloves, grated

1 tbsp (1 g) fresh cilantro leaves, finely chopped

1 tbsp (15 ml) fresh lemon juice

Sea salt and freshly cracked black pepper, to taste

These crispy, protein-rich black-eyed pea fritters make a fantastic starter or side, and they can easily become the star of your meal when you serve them with roasted veggies or a colorful salad. You can even make them smaller for a quick, tasty party canape!

Transfer the beans and potato into a large bowl and roughly mash them with a fork or potato masher. Add in the green onions, corn, parsley, garlic, zucchini, oat flour and paprika, then season with sea salt and freshly cracked black pepper to taste. If the mixture is too wet, add an extra tablespoon (8 g) of oat flour.

Heat 1 inch (2.5 cm) of oil in a small skillet over medium heat. Shape the vegetable mixture into small patties, then add them, a few at a time, into the hot oil. Cook them undisturbed for 2 minutes on each side, or until they are nicely crispy and golden brown.

Remove them with a slotted spoon, and transfer them to a plate covered with paper towels to absorb the excess oil. Repeat the process with the remaining patties, then transfer them onto a large serving plate.

For the garlic dip, pour the yogurt into a bowl, then add the garlic, cilantro and lemon juice. Season with a pinch of sea salt and freshly cracked black pepper. Serve alongside the fritters.

Quick Beetroot Hummus Dip

1 cooked beetroot, peeled and chopped

½ (7-oz [200-g]) can chickpeas, rinsed and drained

1 tbsp (15 g) tahini

1 garlic clove, minced

Zest and juice of ½ lemon

1 tbsp (15 ml) extra-virgin oil

1 tsp za'atar spice mix

1 tbsp (6 g) fresh mint leaves, minced, plus 1 tbsp (6 g), chopped, for garnish

Sea salt and freshly cracked black pepper, to taste

1 tsp black sesame seeds, for garnish

This quick beetroot hummus recipe makes a wonderful and easy appetizer or snack to share. It's refreshing, beautifully smooth and nutritious; it pairs well with both veggie crudités and tortilla chips; and it's just as great smothered inside a sandwich. To speed up the process, buy cooked beets that are vacuum-packed, and save yourself the time of cooking them yourself. You can easily find them with the produce or in the refrigerated aisle in grocery stores.

In a food processor, place the beetroot, chickpeas, tahini, garlic, lemon zest and juice and olive oil.

Blend all the ingredients for about 1 minute, or until the mixture reaches a creamy and smooth consistency.

Add in the za'atar spice mix, mint and season with ¼ teaspoon of sea salt (or to taste) and ¼ teaspoon of freshly cracked black pepper (or to taste). Mix through with a spoon, transfer the hummus into a serving bowl and serve with mint leaves and black sesame seeds on top.

Cooking Tip: *Za'atar is a popular Middle Eastern spice mix loaded with tangy and zesty flavor. If you cannot easily find it, substitute it with a pinch of dried oregano and thyme.*

Broad Bean and Zucchini Meatballs

1 tbsp (15 ml) extra-virgin olive oil

½ onion, finely minced

1 garlic clove, grated

1 small zucchini, finely grated

2 cups (240 g) fresh or frozen broad beans, shelled

3 tbsp (6 g) fresh mint or basil leaves, finely chopped

Zest and juice of ½ lemon

1 tbsp (20 g) sesame seeds

½ tsp fine sea salt

A pinch of freshly cracked black pepper

¾ cup (69 g) chickpea flour

Vegetable oil, for frying

Broad beans (also known as fava beans), chickpea flour and veggies blended together deliver delicious little green balls packed with good-for-you ingredients. They make a tasty game-day snack, and they're definitely delicious served as a main alongside roasted veggies, potato mash and a salad.

Heat the olive oil in a large pan over medium heat, then add the onion, garlic and zucchini and stir-fry for 3 to 4 minutes, until the zucchini loses some moisture, then turn the heat off.

Transfer the zucchini mixture to a food processor. Add the beans, mint, lemon zest and juice, sesame seeds, sea salt and freshly cracked black pepper, then pulse until reaching a thick paste, stopping to scrape the sides of the food processor if necessary. Add the chickpea flour, then pulse again to combine all the ingredients.

Use your hands or an ice cream scoop to form small balls or patties. If the mixture is too wet, add an extra tablespoon (6 g) of chickpea flour. If it's too dry, add a tablespoon (15 ml) of water.

Heat 3 inches (8 cm) of oil in a small pot over medium heat until it reaches 350°F (175°C).

Add in a few balls and let them cook, turning them around until they are crispy and golden brown on all sides.

Remove them with a slotted spoon and transfer them onto a plate covered with paper towels to absorb the excess oil. Repeat the process with the remaining balls, then transfer them onto a large serving plate and serve.

> Cooking Tip: *If you have unshelled broad beans, simply blanch them for a couple of minutes, then remove and discard their outer shells.*

Extra Creamy Classic Hummus

1 (15.5-oz [440-g]) can chickpeas, rinsed and drained

1½ tsp (7 g) baking soda

2 tbsp (30 g) tahini

1 garlic clove, grated

2 tbsp (30 ml) fresh lemon juice

A pinch of fine sea salt

1 tbsp (15 ml) extra-virgin oil

A pinch of za'atar spice mix (optional)

A pinch of smoked paprika

Classic hummus never goes out of fashion! The popular Middle Eastern dip makes a wonderful snack and takes very little time to prepare. It's perfect for dipping crunchy veggies and toasted pita bread, or smothered over my Spring-Perfect Socca Pizza (page 117) or my Green Veggie Chickpea Burger (page 51).

Place the chickpeas beans in a large bowl, cover them with warm water and stir in the baking soda. Allow them to soak for 5 minutes, then rub them together to easily peel their skin off. Discard the peels, rinse and drain the beans well, then transfer them in the bowl of a food processor.

Blend the chickpeas until you reach a thick crumbly texture, about 2 minutes, scraping down the sides of the bowl when necessary.

Add in the tahini, garlic, lemon juice and a generous pinch of sea salt, then blend all the ingredients until smooth, about 3 to 4 minutes. Taste to adjust the seasoning, adding more sea salt and fresh lemon juice as needed.

Transfer the hummus into a serving bowl, drizzle with olive oil and season with za'atar and paprika and serve.

> Cooking Tip: *To help you achieve a super creamy and smooth texture, try adding one ice cube into the food processor together with the other ingredients—I know it sounds odd but it helps!*

Movie Popcorn-Like Chickpeas

1 (15.5-oz [440-g]) can chickpeas, rinsed and drained

1½ tsp (3 g) rosemary leaves, minced

1 garlic clove, grated

A pinch of za'atar spice mix

1½ tbsp (25 ml) extra-virgin oil

Sea salt and freshly cracked black pepper, to taste

Did you know that canned chickpeas can be easily transformed into a super crunchy, super tasty and highly nutritious snack? Next time you're in the mood for a movie, ditch the popcorn and grab a bowl of crispy oven-roasted chickpeas—you'll be amazed!

Preheat the oven to 430°F (220°C) and arrange the baking rack onto the middle shelf.

Place the chickpeas on paper towels and pat them dry, removing any loose skin.

Line a baking tray with parchment paper, add the chickpeas, rosemary, garlic, za'atar, olive oil and ¼ teaspoon (or to taste) of sea salt. Toss all the ingredients well with a spoon to evenly coat the chickpeas, then spread them in a single layer.

Transfer the tray to the oven and roast the chickpeas for 30 to 40 minutes, stirring them halfway through the baking time, until they are golden brown and crunchy.

Remove the chickpeas from the oven, season with a pinch of freshly cracked black pepper and serve.

Cooking Tip: *Once you have mastered the recipe, get crazy with the spices! Garam masala, sumac, chili powder or cayenne pepper are all great options to flavor your popcorn chickpeas.*

Delicious Desserts You Won't Believe Are Made with Beans

If you're looking for a healthier weeknight dessert (I mean . . . who isn't?), this chapter is for you!

I know that legume-based desserts might sound a bit weird at first, but beans are a mighty force when it comes to maximizing the nutritional value of your sweet treats. The best part is, they go completely undetected, so no one will ever guess these desserts are made with beans (not even the picky eaters in your family!).

From Fudgy Adzuki Bean Brownies (page 144) and PB & Chickpea Chocolate Chip Cookies (page 139) to Black Bean Chocolate Pudding (page 143) and Banana Bread with a Pulse Twist (page 140), this chapter includes all my favorite bean desserts with healthy twists that don't sacrifice the flavor. Get ready to stock your pantry with beans, because these treats are so delicious that you'll never want to run out of legumes ever again!

Butter Bean-licious Cookie Dough

⅔ cup (60 g) rolled oats

⅔ cup (60 g) almond flour

4 tbsp (60 ml) unsweetened almond milk

1 tbsp (15 g) almond butter or another nut butter

⅓ cup (65 g) coconut sugar

¼ cup (60 ml) pure maple syrup

1 tsp pure vanilla extract

¼ tsp sea salt flakes

1 (15.5-oz [440-g]) can butter beans, rinsed and drained

1 tbsp (10 g) vegan dark chocolate chips

TO SERVE

Mixed fruit, chopped (optional)

Cookies or crackers (optional)

Butter bean cookie dough. Yep, this is real! Who knew that blending butter beans with a bunch of wholesome ingredients would deliver a rich cookie batter that tastes just like dessert but is sneakily loaded with plant-based protein? Remember that this "dough" is not meant to be baked—it should just be enjoyed as a snack or as a dip. I hope you have your spoon ready, because this faux-dough is bean-licious!

Place the rolled oats and the almond flour in the bowl of a food processor and pulse for 30 seconds, or until the oats are ground into a powder-like consistency. Add the almond milk, almond butter, coconut sugar, maple syrup, vanilla and sea salt into the bowl of the food processor, then add the butter beans.

Blend all the ingredients on medium speed until smooth, scraping down the sides of the bowl if necessary. If the mixture is too thick, pour in 1 tablespoon (15 ml) of almond milk at a time until you reach the desired consistency. If, for some reason, the dough is too creamy, add in an extra tablespoon (6 g) of almond flour at a time, until you reach the desired consistency.

Transfer the cookie dough into a serving bowl, and mix in the dark chocolate chips. Serve it with your favorite chopped fruit, cookies or crackers.

> Cooking Tip: *You can safely freeze this bean cookie dough into small freezer-friendly storage containers for up to 1 month. Let it thaw in the refrigerator overnight and give it a nice stir before serving.*

Chocolate Hummus Dip

1 (15.5-oz [440-g]) can chickpeas, rinsed and drained

4 tbsp (60 ml) unsweetened almond milk

4 tbsp (60 ml) maple syrup

4 tbsp (20 g) unsweetened cocoa powder

2 tsp (10 ml) pure vanilla extract

¼ tsp sea salt flakes

1 tbsp (10 g) vegan dark chocolate chips

TO SERVE

Fruit

Cookies

Crackers

A nutritious chocolate hummus dip that is easy to make and ready in less than five minutes? Count me in! This healthier chocolate spread makes a wonderful snack for the whole family, including kids, and you can serve it up with all your favorite fruit for a nutritional boost.

Place the chickpeas in the bowl of a food processor, then add the milk, maple syrup, cocoa powder, vanilla and sea salt.

Blend all the ingredients on medium speed until smooth, scraping down the sides of the bowl if necessary. If the mixture is too thick, pour in 1 tablespoon (15 ml) of almond milk at a time until you reach the desired consistency.

Transfer the chocolate hummus into a serving bowl and mix in the dark chocolate chips. Serve with your favorite fruit, cookies or crackers.

PB & Chickpea Chocolate Chip Cookies

1 (15.5-oz [440-g]) can chickpeas, rinsed and drained

½ cup (130 g) unsalted peanut butter

4 tbsp (60 g) coconut sugar

¼ cup (25 g) gluten-free oat flour

1 tsp pure vanilla extract

1½ tsp (7 g) baking soda

A pinch of sea salt flakes

4 tbsp (40 g) vegan dark chocolate chips

A healthy cookie recipe that's easy and fun to make with the kids? Yes, please! Loaded with plant-based protein and conveniently gluten-free, these healthy cookies make a great lunchbox addition and a fantastic afternoon snack!

Preheat oven to 360°F (180°C) and arrange the baking rack onto the middle shelf.

Place the chickpeas and peanut butter in the bowl of a food processor, and blend on medium speed until smooth, scraping down the sides of the bowl if necessary.

Add in the coconut sugar, oat flour, vanilla, baking soda and salt and pulse to combine all the ingredients, then stir in the chocolate chips.

Use an ice cream scoop with a spring release or a spoon to drop the cookies onto a baking tray covered with parchment paper.

Flatten each cookie ball just a tiny bit with the palm of your hand or the back of a spoon.

Place the baking tray in the oven, and bake for about 12 minutes, or until they look golden and crunchy on the outside.

Take the cookies out of the oven, allow them to cool and then serve.

Cooking Tip: *For a nice little twist, you can also swap peanut butter for almond or cashew butter and use vegan white chocolate chips.*

Banana Bread with a Pulse Twist

3 large bananas, mashed

⅓ cup (80 ml) coconut oil, melted

¼ cup (60 ml) almond or oat milk

½ cup (120 ml) maple syrup or coconut sugar

1 tsp pure vanilla extract

1⅓ cups (120 g) chickpea flour

1 cup (120 g) whole wheat flour

2 tsp (10 g) baking powder

1 tsp ground cinnamon

A pinch of ground nutmeg

A pinch of sea salt

3 tbsp (45 g) raw walnuts or pecans, chopped

4 tbsp (40 g) vegan dark chocolate chips

For me, it's not Sunday morning without a hot tea and thick slice of banana bread. I've been trying to add a nutritional boost to my vegan banana bread for the past couple years, and I've had the most amazing result simply by replacing some of the flour with chickpea flour—a super easy swap that brings in some extra nutritional value. Best of all, it tastes delicious, so it's a win-win!

Preheat oven to 360°F (180°C) and arrange the baking rack onto the middle shelf.

In a large bowl, whisk together the bananas, coconut oil, almond milk, maple syrup and vanilla.

In another bowl, mix together the chickpea flour with the whole wheat flour, baking powder, cinnamon, nutmeg and sea salt.

Slowly incorporate the dry ingredients into the wet ones and mix until just combined. Add in the walnuts and chocolate chips and gently stir until combined.

Transfer the mixture into a 10-inch x 5-inch (25-cm x 13-cm) loaf tin covered with parchment paper, then level the batter surface with a spoon. Bake in the oven for 40 to 45 minutes, or until the loaf is golden on top. Check for doneness by inserting a toothpick into the center. If it comes out clean, the banana bread is ready.

Remove from the oven, allow to cool completely, then transfer the banana bread onto a serving plate and serve.

Cooking Tip: *For a nice little twist, you can also swap dark chocolate chips with white chocolate chips and replace walnuts with roasted pecans or almonds.*

Black Bean Chocolate Pudding

1 (15-oz [425-g]) can black beans, rinsed and drained

¼ cup (60 ml) coconut milk

2 tbsp (20 g) roasted hazelnuts

4 tbsp (20 g) unsweetened cocoa powder

4 tbsp (60 ml) maple syrup

2 medjool dates, pitted

2 tbsp (30 ml) coconut oil, melted

1 tsp pure vanilla extract

This incredibly easy and delicious vegan chocolate pudding has a secret power ingredient: black beans! Don't worry though; they go absolutely undetected and the result is a creamy, luscious and healthier chocolate treat for any time of the day.

Add the black beans and coconut milk into a powerful blender and blend on medium speed until the beans are completely pureed, scraping down the sides of the blender if necessary.

Add the hazelnuts, cocoa powder, maple syrup, dates, coconut oil and vanilla into the blender and blend all the ingredients until creamy and smooth.

Divide the pudding into four individual pots, refrigerate them until set, about 1 hour, then serve.

> Cooking Tip: *Have fun with the toppings! Here are some yummy favorite ideas: vegan whipped cream, strawberries, roasted nuts and dark chocolate shavings.*

Fudgy Adzuki Bean Brownies

1 cup (300 g) sweetened adzuki bean paste

1 tbsp (15 ml) coconut oil, melted

¼ cup (60 ml) maple syrup or coconut sugar

1 tsp pure vanilla extract

¼ cup (20 g) unsweetened cocoa powder

¼ cup (30 g) all-purpose flour

½ tsp baking powder

½ tsp baking soda

A pinch of sea salt

4 tbsp (40 g) vegan dark chocolate chips

Craving brownies but looking for something just a little bit healthier? I've got you covered! These fudgy treats call for adzuki beans, which work well to make soft, gooey brownies, and they also supply healthy amounts of protein and fiber!

Preheat the oven to 360°F (180°C) and arrange the baking rack onto the middle shelf.

Place the adzuki bean paste, coconut oil, maple syrup, vanilla and cocoa powder in a food processor and blend until combined. Add in the flour, baking powder, baking soda and sea salt. Pulse until just combined, then stir in the chocolate chips.

Transfer the brownie batter into 6-inch (15-cm) square baking pan covered with parchment paper and level the surface with a spoon. Bake in the oven for 20 to 30 minutes, or until the edges are set and the center is still slightly jiggly.

Remove the brownies from the oven and allow them to cool completely. Transfer onto a cooling rack and allow it to set completely, then cut into squares and serve.

Cooking Tip: *Adzuki bean paste is already sweetened, so if you can't easily find adzuki bean paste, you can substitute with the same amount of black beans and add 2 extra tablespoons (30 ml) of maple syrup.*

Acknowledgments

To Jenna and the whole team at Page Street Publishing, for believing in me once again and allowing me to create this wonderful cookbook.

To Oscar, my biggest fan and supporter. Dad, I love you so much.

To Noah, my little coworker, thank you for helping Mama measure the ingredients for the recipes, holding food styling props and giving a little taste here and there. You made this whole cookbook a lot more fun to create. I love you.

To my family, for being the best cheerleaders I could ask for.

To Valerio, my official taste tester, critic, tripod-holder, last-minute supermarket-trips-runner and best partner-in-crime I could ask for.

To Simone, for helping me test, double test, triple test and troubleshoot all the recipes in this cookbook. Your help made my book ten times better.

To all my friends, for your honest feedback through all the recipes you have tested and for cooking for me when I just couldn't bear the thought of cooking for the millionth time in a day.

Finally, a big thank you to all the home cooks, chefs and foodies of the world. Thank you for being so passionate and sharing your love with the world. Food helps us connect with each other in so many ways, and I'm forever grateful to be part of this community.

About the Author

Andrea Soranidis is the founder, writer and photographer behind the popular food blog The Petite Cook, which was nominated as a finalist in the UK Brilliance in Blogging awards. She is also the author of *20-Minute Italian*, published in 2019. She was born and raised in Sicily—one of the most enchanting islands of Italy—and now splits her time between London, Sicily and Germany.

The Petite Cook has been her creative outlet since 2014, where she still shares all the traditional Italian recipes she grew up with, as well as her kitchen experiments inspired by travels around the world. Visit www.thepetitecook.com for more cooking inspiration.

Index